Tough Choices

Reflections of an Afrikaner African

Van Zyl Slabbert

TAFELBERG

First published in 1999 under the title *Afrikaner Afrikaan*

© 2000 Frederik Van Zyl Slabbert
Tafelberg Publishers Limited, 28 Wale Street, Cape Town 8001

All rights reserved. No part of this book may be
reproduced or transmitted in any form or by any
means, electronic or mechanical, including
photocopying, recording or any information
storage and retrieval system, without permission
in writing from the publisher.

Translated from the Afrikaans by Tania Slabbert
Cover design by Simon Ford
Typography and design by Etienne van Duyker,
ALINEA STUDIO, Cape Town
Printed and bound by NBD, Drukkery Street,
Goodwood, Western Cape
First edition, first impression 2000

ISBN 0 624 03880 7

DEDICATED
To Comrade J.I.K Gagiano:
From your old friend with the bends

THANK YOU
To Marga Collings, who edited meticulously, and in the kindest manner. Especially to Hannes van Zyl, without whose nagging and support this book would never have seen the light of day. To Breyten, for his words of abuse, comfort and introduction. And to my daughter, Tania, for all the hard work in translating the manuscript into readable English.

Contents

Fire in the Fingers: A Foreword 9

Prologue: Full Circle 19

1 Mind Shaping 27
2 The Last White Parliament 39
3 Relationships and Coincidences 52
4 Birthmarks 72
5 Does the Boer Make the Plan or the Plan Make the Boer? 90
6 The Struggle 97
7 The New in the Old and the Old in the New 112
8 Truth without Reconciliation, Reconciliation without Truth 131

Epilogue: The Here and Now 148

Fire in the Fingers: A Foreword

IT IS MY PRIVILEGE TO WELCOME Van Zyl Slabbert into the circle of Philistines, know-it-alls and unwavering tremblers – in other words, writers. To put it this way may sound condescending: he has, after all, often put pen to paper to express his thoughts; he has abundantly cherished his history in words. But I make bold to argue that this present collection of essays, reflections and narratives is his first real book as a writer, in part because a grappling with language takes place here as well.

The process of writing creates its own space, a sphere of influence that grows as the writing expands. It is a thread of experience and consciousness and because it seeks a continuous battle with the tools of experience – words, concepts, the spaces and rhythms and perceptions and, therefore, the history of a specific language – it is also an ongoing revolution, an assault on the language itself. We are shaped (and entertained!) by our attempts to define the boundaries of reality by means of these tools of experience, perhaps even the hubris of our desire to *change* institutions and relationships. We want to bend the language to meet our needs, and we are moulded by the nature of the language in which we work.

A generally accepted statement about modernism is that the nature of language depicts *form* rather than embracing *content*. In our case we know that this language, Afrikaans – with its history and connotations, its spaces and passages, its 'echoes', one might say – is currently undergoing a turnabout/transition. It will therefore shift and, hopefully liberated from negative contexts, can now live 'freely', dependent only on its own ability to map out a *raison d'être*. In a certain sense we have been winnowed out of the greater power play. Our relationship towards power has perhaps changed. Where does this leave us? The will to comprehend is, after all, not the same as the will to possess.

But is this all? Are we only winding up the ledger? Is Van Zyl now merely an aesthete? Or someone who just wants to bring his own history into view? Meaning is continuously created and patched together, whether we like it or not – even if it is only through the intellectual equivalent of negative space.

Where does language stand in relation to power? Is language (that is, writing) a power in its own right, a possible undermining of the state's heavy arbitrary machinery of doctrine (sometimes ideology) and administration? Or is it just another weapon for the political bosses, the bourgeoisie of the stock exchange and the commonalty of academia, the cultural and religious establishment? We have lived through both strategies in our time: Afrikaans was at once the excuse and reinforcement for the utter perversion of racial *baasskap*, and the heartbeat that helped to burst the congested Afrikaner arteries.

In former innocence some of us believed that power was a singular entity, depicted in the dichotomy between those who possessed it and those who had nothing. Now we know that, on the one hand, it is an ideological construct that manifests itself in all institutions and, on the other, it is a many-headed phenomenon – the devils in the details and the crush-pens – which is present in even the most delicate mechanisms of social interaction, both publicly and privately. Power is a quotient in any form and manner of association. And everywhere there are 'empowered' voices that would presume to manipulate the discourse of power. One even finds it in the supposed resistance to power! Roland Barthes, the French master of semiotics, once put it as follows: 'I consider the discourse of power to be any discourse that apportions blame and thus fosters guilt in the one to whom it is ascribed.'

It has always been this way. A revolution occurs to burst the veins of the fossilised monolith, to overthrow the old dispensation, to apportion power like multiplied breads and fishes to the previously disadvantaged – and, like *kakiebos*, the transgressions and abuses of power blossom in the new democratic playing fields.

And the conductor of power is the language that we speak and write, because we forget that any expression is a classification, and every grouping is oppressive: *ordo* means both dispersion and threat. But a bird is known by its song and a man by his talk. The language philosopher Jakobson (who claimed that language was law) pointed out that a language system is recognised not so much by what it allows us to say but by what it forces us to say ...

As one-eyed wind jackal (and in my capacity as a philosidiot) I am taking this roundabout route to show that Van Zyl Slabbert's writing (*all* writing) contains ambiguities, uncertainties and confusion, but also delicious illuminations and pleasures. There is a danger attached to thoughts. He plays with fire: playing with fire can get your fingers burnt, but it also burns the wounds clean and even brings some light into the tunnel.

Since he has now brought his ostrich eggshell filled with glowing coals into the circle of moaners and seekers, one might remind him that the writer regards the self as his calling and life as a reading of the self. Because the most personal is also the most undermining and, paradoxically, the most common. He knows this, of course, which is why this book reads like the narrative of a personal journey. That is good: in this era of decay and artificiality we attach more value to an account of a personally experienced trajectory than to grandiose analyses and principles.

Nevertheless, since time immemorial the writer has also been preoccupied with the desire – no, the *need* – to represent something. What? In the last instance, just as in the first: that which is genuine, that which is real. ('Reality is perhaps merely an illusion/trick of the mind, but it is the only place where one can get a steak,' said Woody Allen.) You know you can never fully incarnate it; literature is, as a matter of fact, the result of the quest for the unattainable. But then we also know that it has to do with the quality of the journey and the texture of our lives and not the destination as such. Because there is in any case no doubt that the Great Bear is patiently waiting for us, and only whistles softly to us every now and then so that we do not stray too far from the path in our wanderings – and how we deliberately feign ignorance sometimes! Our writings are informed by the life around us, by the times we live in and through and around which we move. And part of that 'time' and 'environment' are all the other lives we lead.

In European cities one often sees bronze plaques or ceramic tiles built into the façades of houses to mark the birthplace or residence of an illustrious personage. (We are unlikely to find this in Moerland because we have not yet reached consensus about who and what is worthy and we know nothing of a shared heritage that prevails above all other divisions.) And so I recently read on the wall of a house in Poble Gran, our market town where I buy fish to keep the Great Bear happy in the interim: *En aquesta casa hi visqué* (then the name follows) – *pensador i escriptor i pedagog i politic.* (Here lived X – thinker, writer, pedagogue and politician.) And I thought to myself that, except for a few words, one could say much the same about Van Zyl's protean life. Except that to be complete one would have to add: businessman, sports fanatic, at times a drinker of stature before the Almighty, do-gooder, adviser, facilitator, chairman of a range of institutions (in fact, a veteran sitter on chairs), mediator, meat and wine connoisseur ... The rest, and there is much, the reader will encounter in this bundle of essays.

The pages that follow are scattered with his quest for the comprehensible and the acceptable as much as with his rejection of anything that smacks of nonsense or empty rhetoric. He is an empirical thinker (also compelling and incisive) and a realist. At times even a voluntarist. (But then one remembers that a volunteer is free-willed and that the noun 'voluntary' describes both a piece of music and a supporter of the independence of the church.)

I got to know Van Zyl Slabbert to some extent when he visited me in prison in his then capacity as opposition leader. He appealed to The Man with the Threatening Forefinger to grant permission for my wife to pay me a contact visit, and argued for my release. In those days, prisons were not what they have since become. Parole was basically unthinkable, the chances of release were slim (not to mention escape), and the men with the pig brains in control were inflexible. I never received the contact visit but ultimately Van Zyl's concern with my fate was the overwhelming factor in my 'early' release.

Thereafter I got to know him better during visits to Paris. The juice that flows from the vine opens up and cleanses dumb hearts. On the first two occasions that we met he was still a member of Parliament and I accompanied him to various meetings overseas with foreign affairs at the Quai d'Orsay or with other interest groups who wanted to be informed about South Africa. Through his analyses I came to understand the complexities of the situation better. In our discussions he did not hide the fact that he had become disillusioned by the futility of parliamentary processes. But his decision to resign from the ranks of the hypocrites and the fools was nevertheless a surprise.

On more than one occasion he would in future years help me out of trouble. I remember that thanks to his intervention I could even obtain a visa, issued with grotesque conditions attached, to visit my dying father for the last time. Presumably Van Zyl personally had to guarantee that I would not cause trouble. At the consulate in Mbabane he had to draw the route that we would take by car on a map. And together we entered the wonderful country, going ever south along the Lesotho border, through snow and deserted mountain passes, through the wretchedness of a ravished Ciskei, to Grahamstown where Oubaas lay waiting with a grey face, dark eyes and paralysed hands for the Great Bear.

We would eventually take on more than one utopia together, although I must add that I did most of the shouting while Van Zyl had to find the means to make the dream a reality. This was how it became possible to arrange the Dakar expedition, the first genuine and public political meeting between sixty-odd passport-bearers from South Africa – all people with influence in their various fields – and the banned African National Congress; probably the start of the thawing process which helped pave the way for a negotiated settlement. A few years later, we could set up the Gorée Institute on the old slave island in the bay of Dakar: as a pan-African institution for research, reflection and creativity, to promote democratic processes, economic development, the empowerment of communities and the development of cultural activities on our continent.

This shift from the local to a wider context is characteristic of Van Zyl's searching and visionary spirit. For him it is a given that we as Afrikaners (with our heritage from Europe and the East) are inextricably part of Africa and that we therefore have certain responsibilities and duties – in the first instance to try to *understand* our shared history and environment, to *know* how historical injustices arose and *who* was responsible and *who* benefited from the perks and privileges – and that we possess specific skills and capabilities that can only achieve their potential and be fully exploited within the African context. We are already living in this greater here and now; just as we are *in* and *from* Africa, so Africa through all her diverse and sometimes gruesome expressions determines how we see and come to grips with life and the world. We are Afrikaner-Africans.

Have we turned the corner yet? Given the nature of developments since 1990, the shift in views and the partial transformation of structures in Moerland, it is clear that Van Zyl's pragmatic approach was better equipped to interpret the situation than my own utopian highs and pessimistic lows. In a transition (as opposed to a revolution) one had to take into account existing structures; the 'better instincts' of key people within those entities had to be encouraged in order to prevent chaos and implosion, and to facilitate and speed up the handing over of power. This was the very least that the economic sector, as stabiliser of everyday life, demanded as guarantee for its continued activities. This then meant that, in a first phase at least, one could not destabilise those structures (largely controlled and managed by Afrikaners). Furthermore, it was simply realistic not to drive the Afrikaners into a reactionary cul-de-sac by defeating them completely. This was of course the line taken by the ANC, or at least by the decision-making faction within the movement.

Whether or not that 'line' will become the rope around the Afrikaner's neck – or even the rope that the ANC trips over – remains to be seen. In any event we cannot go back; the apple with the bite in it cannot be 'unbitten'. Somebody once said that in South Africa, 'the worst never happens'. Our political culture, which is English, depends, at least on the surface, on a muddling through which brings into being its own rhythm, reason for existence and environment.

Van Zyl would probably agree with me that an historical compromise between two power blocs – the former and the replacer, because I do not wish to say the 'old' and the 'new' since there is too much that is 'old' within the ANC – is still far removed from 'nation-building'. Even if this should perhaps also be a prerequisite. I still believe that there should be a revolutionary propulsion towards transformation, and that in this process deeper reflection is necessary about the unlocking dynamics of the creative interaction between cultures, the way in which together they transform each other, and the fact that in remarkable fashion we – as individuals and groups – are people with plural identities. But for this process, which needs to be *driven* to make it realisable, our leaders are far too lazy and arrogant, and most Afrikaners are too scared and small-minded. We could all yet live to regret this.

Another result of the above process, and one which actually took place, was surely that the central and centralising functions of the state as we formerly knew it were never questioned. On the contrary, that in this regard we are now experiencing the same obtuseness and arrogance, and a similar overlap of ruling party and state, in the new order as when the National Party was in control. We are truly becoming a one-party state and the party *is* the state. This is what happened in Mexico, Algeria and Vietnam following their respective revolutions, with the results that we see today. Would 'another path' have offered better results? Would Vietnam have been less poor and backward, would Mexico have found a solution to achieving the integration and participation of the majority Indian population in national life, would Algeria have been spared the strangulation of a bloody civil war caused by the corruption of the 'liberator state'? Given their specific situations of extreme poverty with chasms between the poor and the privileged, and the explosive ethnic and cultural make-up of their populations – would a robust democracy with strong counterchecks have worked better for them or not? Or would the total implementation of a democratic system merely have led to chaos, a battle for power between various warlords and, on top of that, the destabilising activities of those previously in power? Who knows?

South Africa is a melting pot or concentrate of problems that are also becoming more acute elsewhere in the world, and that is why our possible 'solutions' are important and exemplary. South Africa is a survival option, the 'less worse' alternative. South Africa is a construct: because it is the result of dreams, just as much as of thoughts and deeds; because it is 'in the making' (I do not think we are even close to finding our final *form*); because it largely escapes ordered and stereotyped classifications; because it is a dangerous puzzle; because we constantly need to repeat the words so as not to lose their taste in our mouths; because it needs to keep on moving as stalling would lead to polarisation and confrontation. In such a melting pot, the will to understanding is important, but so is striving towards rebuilding (which I personally would extend to metamorphosis). This is why the dialectic is so necessary, the shaping and creating effect of exchange, confrontation and co-ordination.

We are all different. Is there even, strictly speaking, a commonality among whitish Afrikaners? Van Zyl shows us that that 'blueprint' has finally been broken, that there have always been 'alternative' Afrikaners, that Afrikaners as a group can therefore not all be hauled over the same guilty coals, that it is 'normal' to be 'different'.

The link that I tried to establish above (and about which Van Zyl and I have debated for years) puts concepts like identity and language and ethics in a new light. We need to develop a finer sense of what is 'own' and what is 'shared', and the knowledge that the one cannot exist without the other, and that the fluctuating and changing comparisons are a prerequisite for development, and that development – that is, a refinement of knowledge and insight – is a *sine qua non* for survival. For true survival.

It is here that Van Zyl Slabbert's voice is so important. Because what he brings to us in different tones is an account of a search for greater clarity from which we can all benefit, and the result of a spiritual and intellectual journey which, thanks to the ethical horizons that frame the journey, can serve as an example and an inspiration for us all.

And because I value his friendship, I wish to end where I began by repeating that it is a privilege for me to preface his book and to introduce his words. May other Afrikaans-speakers be inspired by this book to also tell of their experiences and thoughts so that we, enriched by our peculiarities and differences, together can gather the essential *padkos* for the onward journey. Let the road sing!

Breyten Breytenbach
Can Ocells, July 1999

Prologue: Full Circle

> *Such knowledge is too wonderful for me;*
> *it is high, I cannot attain it.*
> — PSALM 139 VERSE 6

EARLY ON WEEKDAY MORNINGS I lie in bed, waiting for the radio alarm to sound so that I can listen to the six o'clock news. At five to six every morning there is a message from one religion or another. Jewish on Mondays, then Christian, Muslim, Hindu, and so on. It always astounds me how easily the preachers talk about God and His thoughts; each one of them convinced that he or she knows how everything fits together. As soon as I begin to think about these things I get caught up in basic ontological problems, which affect my thoughts on so many matters. For example: the idea of God implies consciousness, awareness, will, a plan. God's love, mercy, wrath, and so forth, are talked about freely, but never God's head or brain. And this is where my dilemma begins.

I cannot accept the notion of a brainless consciousness. For me it is already 'too wonderful' that my brain – a describable, jellyfish-like lump in my head, with neurons, dendrons, synapses, and so on – is responsible for an invisible consciousness that allows me to experience a self. Is it a 'self' that is writing right now? Without hands I cannot write, but there is another 'self' that can think. But without a consciousness there cannot be a self that can think. Or can there be a selfless consciousness? Perhaps with artificial intelligence. There can even be a brain without consciousness. It cannot think or experience a self. But a brainless consciousness? Ultimately, the apparatus – the brain and senses – is indispensable. It is the material basis for consciousness. But consciousness is more important than the apparatus, because without consciousness I cannot even know that I am. Something can be more important than that which is indispensable, because that something helps you to understand that something else is indispensable.

What lies on the other side of consciousness? If my apparatus is the portal to the experience of reality, is reality real or just a construct of my consciousness? This philosophical mystery has yet to be finally unravelled. One simply takes a stand and starts arguing from that position. I believe there is a reality outside of my consciousness, but I would not be able to prove or explain it. My consciousness breaks that reality up into digestible bites by means of my experience of the moment. But it is never an isolated moment. The experience is tempered by my knowledge, emotions and memory; in other words, by the history of my self. The self can never experience total reality at any given moment. That is why my knowledge of reality will always be incomplete, never final.

If this is the case, does it make sense to talk of the progress or advancement of knowledge? I believe so. A person learns from experience and begins to avoid mistakes. What we call science is a way of thinking about reality, and it is the most disciplined dissection of the world that humanity has been capable of to date. This knowledge can be put into words and conveyed in such a manner that more than one person can understand it in the same way. This does not mean that this knowledge is infallible or that it is the final word on anything. It is, however, the basis of technological development and has had by far the greatest common impact on people's experience of reality in the twentieth century. The technological application of scientific knowledge – steam, electricity, atomic energy, antibiotics – has changed people's lives fundamentally. To date, the scientific manner of thinking has been the most culturally transcendental and neutral method available to mankind to explore reality. This fact makes me sceptical about the position of radical relativism, namely that we are individually locked into constructions of our own consciousness and that a shared experience of reality can never be conveyed in a comprehensible manner but is determined by what one is trying to say.

Nevertheless, just as my consciousness can never have a complete grip on reality, so too a scientific analysis of reality can never be a final account of my experience of reality. My experience is infinitely wider and more nuanced than my capacity to give a scientific account of it. It is not just about music, literature or art. It is also about experiencing people, love, relationships, ethics, death, the beauty of nature – things that leave you speechless due to your inability to express what they mean to you. There are times when speaking is the least effective means of communication. But whatever the experience, it is filtered through the portal of my consciousness, and my consciousness is dependent on the good working order of my apparatus – my brain and senses. If my apparatus is not functioning, then I am 'out of my mind' and I am not the 'self' that people know and to whom they react. To see someone who has been brain-damaged through a stroke or sclerosis is to see how consciousness begins to fade away before your eyes.

But let us return to the matter of a brainless consciousness. People who take terms such as 'soul' and 'spirit' literally probably believe in such a consciousness. I find it difficult to grasp. That is why I have a problem with the personification of God, the ascription of personal properties to God as if there were a physical brain. If there is no brain, there can be no consciousness. If there is a brain, it must have the same relationship with consciousness as any other brain has with consciousness. Consequently, that consciousness is also fallible, with an incomplete grasp on reality. But this would make the idea of God unnecessary. The notion remains an unsubstantiated metaphor to me. I can understand why people need God; I even have sympathy with their need. But the fallible knowledge which my apparatus helps me to assemble does not enable me to give personal meaning to the word. This is not to say that it cannot be done, just that it has not happened to my satisfaction thus far. And it is not that I have not tried. If only half the qualities ascribed to God are true, it is infinitely easier for God to find me than for me to find God. And I am not in hiding.

Birth and death seem to me to be the most profound and non-experienced moments of my existence. My consciousness begins functioning shortly after my birth and stops as soon as I die. Until it begins functioning, I have a consciousless brain, and when it stops, I have no consciousness and a dead brain. The scientific manner of thinking can help me to understand how I was born and how I die, but it is incapable of explaining to me logically why this happens. I can even wax poetic about how I die by saying that the jellyfish-like lump in my head disintegrates on the beach of nothingness and is devoured by the snails of eternity. This statement can be translated fairly accurately into a scientific parallel, but no scientific translation is possible for the meaning of birth and death. The journey from birth to death is an individual odyssey. And yet it is the source of a common human existential problem: the coincidence of birth and the inevitability of death. Between these two involuntary moments every person searches for meaning. It is the most basic human condition. One can certainly choose to die sooner than necessary, but one cannot decide not to die at all.

To me, the origins of philosophy, literature, art, music, religion, ethics and morality lie in this quest for meaning. This is why scientific knowledge is not necessarily more important than other forms of knowledge. If one traces the history of humanity's search for meaning across all these terrains, one can only conclude that it is nothing short of heroic. The manner in which a human being with a fallible apparatus defines reality in search of the meaning of existence is simply astounding. It is the source of my own experience of a common humanity. It cuts across cultural, racial, ethnic and gender differences.

There have been times of collapse and failure in the search for meaning; times of large-scale barbarism, dogmatic intolerance, collective prejudice and deliberate exclusion at the expense of others. But it is through humanity's resistance and rebellion against such collapse and failure that the truly heroic comes to the fore. Human beings never stop searching for a better alternative. I have great patience with anyone's search for meaning, but I have absolutely no tolerance for people who take whatever gives meaning to their lives and try to force it upon me as the final answer to the quest. (However well intentioned it might be at five to six in the morning.)

I was not born with these insights and observations, and I have not yet stopped searching. Ultimately, for me it has become one of life's rules that there can never be a final answer to the search for meaning – we will never stop searching for better answers. Consequently, the freedom to search for meaning is, for me, the basis of ethics and morality. The pursuit of individual freedom for each human being is the starting point of my views about politics, social institutions, religion, ideology, and so forth. While I am opposed to any stereotyping, labelling or generalisations that cannot be tested, I am reconciled to the fact that in my own, unique, historical context I must take up a position about being typified as African, Afrikaner, South African, white, liberal, male, and so on. But these are social conventions, which do not deal with the dilemma of self–consciousness–brain. I long ago lost the ability to submit fully to a social identity that has been ascribed to me. When, for example, people refer to me as an Afrikaner, I accept it conditionally for the purposes of discussion, but not as an uncritical identification with a piece of social information which has a self-evident meaning between people and groups. For me there is no such thing as 'the Afrikaner' or 'the history of the Afrikaner'. To be called an Afrikaner is the beginning of a discussion, never the final word.

Much more important than these ruminations concerning the validity of a social identity is the primordial will to survive. To want to live, a person must survive. This means searching for the means that make survival possible. Put simply, not to go hungry. That is why poverty is the single greatest threat to individual freedom. Overcoming this threat is the source of social evolution. It has always been so, from hunter-gatherer to agrarian communities and right up to modern industrial society. Patterns of human interaction find their origins in the will of the individual to survive. Herein lie the origins of family ties, ethnic exclusivity and nationalism, up to and including the modern state with citizenship rights.

The capacity of the individual to survive is significantly strengthened through the evolution of communication, language and the written word. In this way, knowledge is gathered and stored and made available for future generations. This means that the individual does not have to start from scratch in discovering the world and creating reliable knowledge, but has access to this knowledge through oral accounts, books, archives and libraries. There are survival lessons determined outside of the individual's world of experience that can be used to find short cuts in the struggle to survive. In the millennia that preceded us and right up to the present, this process has given rise to civilisations and cultures on islands and continents.

And so I find myself on the continent where, according to available information, human civilisation originated, and I am politically caught up in the history of being an Afrikaner. The absolute coincidence of this remains bewildering. Of course I could walk away from it all if I wished. The diversity and possibilities of human experience make it absurd for me to sacrifice my entire experience of being human for one specific social identity. What is more, so many claims to which I have an aversion are still being made in the name of being an Afrikaner that one could easily write off the whole exercise as too exhausting. But this is easier said than done. In my experience of the world and in trying to make sense of it, my being an Afrikaner is a reality with which I have to live and make peace. It is a social birthmark. I am known by it and I am stereotyped and judged by it. In my experience of self, for as long as I am here, I must come to terms with the reality of being South African, African, Afrikaner and white. And I do not wish to be anywhere else. I have known anonymity, alienation and what it is to feel foreign. Sometimes it is pleasant. But mostly I find myself in the daily ritual of social togetherness, in search of food, humour, love – and, of course, meaning.

Here I am at five to six in the morning, a sceptical non-believer of advanced middle age. When I look back, I see that life is a bunch of anecdotes, some analysis and a great deal of wonderment. When I look ahead, I say to myself, 'Thou dost beset me behind and before, and layest Thy hand upon me ... I praise Thee, for Thou art fearful and wonderful. Wonderful are Thy works! Thou knowest me right well ...' (Psalm 139 verses 5 and 14) If David says God has hands, then God must also have a brain. And so the dilemma begins all over again. I know that all it takes is one hard bump on the apparatus for everything to be over. And then the Great Bear is there, waiting for you.

I sent these thoughts to my old and well-read friend Annie Gagiano, because I value her judgement. She says she finds it all too abstract and insipid and, what is more, it is all so obvious. I tell her this is my best attempt to think ontologically. Especially at around five to six in the morning.

1 Mind Shaping

ONE QUESTION THAT HAS ALWAYS baffled me is: 'And how did you get to be where you are?' I think it is because each time I decided what I no longer wanted to be, and not so much what I wanted to become. But why I made these decisions is not easy to explain; one can only describe the process.

It was on a hot afternoon in late summer that I decided I no longer wanted to become a minister in the Dutch Reformed Church. A two-hour lecture by the professor of dogmatics was under way. A theologically founded article by him, entitled 'Apartheid: The Will of God', was taken very seriously in other South African theological seminaries. In a falsetto voice and in language speckled with Hollandisms, he explained why Karl Barth was a heretic. Barth had spoken of God's general grace, through which newborn children would not go to hell because they could not accept responsibility for their actions, and also because they had not had the opportunity to accept Jesus Christ as their Saviour. The professor said we had to distinguish between God's 'general' and 'specific' grace and that only those who had received God's 'specific' grace in terms of John 3 verse 16 could go to heaven; in other words, only those who believed in Jesus could receive eternal life. Babies were therefore in for a tough time. I remember the intellectual fatigue and emotional aversion that came over me. What intolerable rubbish this was! What on God's earth was I doing here? Those who knew His will – the priests and prophets of the hereafter – filtered God himself out of my consciousness.

This disenchantment did not happen suddenly. I was converted in 1956, when I was in standard eight, with the help of Oom Dries Steyn, at a camp of the Students' Christian Association at Winkelspruit. What my primordial needs for God's compassion and acceptance were is difficult to unravel: maybe a broken home, uncertainty about my acceptance, a need for admiration or fellow-believers. Whatever the case, my motives were sincere. Before I reached matric I had carefully read the Bible twice from cover to cover to find out what God wanted to say to me. I went to church twice every Sunday – but only after I had taught Sunday school classes, done missionary work at the hospital in the afternoon and sung hallelujahs before dinner. I studied the Bible every day and attended prayer meetings once a week. I preached the hind leg off a donkey at every opportunity. My friends, with whom I had previously stolen fruit, played rugby and chased girls, thought I had gone mad. Especially when I painstakingly went to each of the houses from which I had stolen fruit – as much as two years before – to beg forgiveness. Many of the people to whom I apologised also thought I was crazy. But I had to be purified before God and my fellow-man.

In matric, religion took up so much of my time that I began wondering whether it was not perhaps my vocation to enter the ministry. My aunt in Johannesburg, with whom my sister and I spent holidays, arranged a meeting with Professor Ben Marais of the theological faculty in Pretoria to give me guidance. He personally did not offer much guidance, but I found the moment so overwhelming – a professor of God before me – that I decided this was a sign that I was called upon to become a minister.

During my first year at Wits, 1959, my life consisted of

Greek, Latin and private Hebrew lessons. In between there was a bit of rugby, but I studied myself to a standstill. That was why I took Afrikaans–Nederlands and sociology as 'soft options'. My first bit of political awareness came when the Fellowship Society organised a lunchtime lecture by Robert Sobukwe of the Pan-Africanist Congress. The hall was packed when he and approximately four hundred blacks loudly proclaimed that they were ready to rule South Africa *now*. It was the strangest idea I had heard in a long time. The Sharpeville march happened soon afterwards, but still I had not really grasped the political situation in South Africa. To me, black people were primarily the sick people in hospital beds to whom I preached the Word of God, or people who worked for us. Except, of course, for the buddies with whom I had grown up on the farm – but that was long before my conversion.

In 1960 I went to Stellenbosch, or rather to Wilgenhof, because this hostel believed that very little at the university existed outside its *esprit de corps*. Wilgenhof was what sociologist Erving Goffman referred to as a 'total institution': it ruled your entire life and required absolute loyalty. During their first two weeks there, students experienced the most intense orientation/initiation/abuse imaginable, both physically and mentally. Strangely, this emphasised independence of thought in particular. Every time you unthinkingly carried out an order, you had to shout 'parrot' repeatedly. At the same time it was drummed into you that 'the place' was an institution that required almost unconditional loyalty. Paradoxically, this strengthened independence.

Wilgenhof was definitely the start of my secularisation. And then, of course, there was sociology, as taught by Dian Joubert. Through him I was introduced to the human-based normativity of our behaviour, I learned that ethics was grounded in society and social life, and that the validity of values was socially based. For someone from the Northern Transvaal (now the Northern Province), firmly convinced that God inspired every thought and action and also provided one with eternally relevant knowledge, this was disconcerting information. The combination of Wilgenhof and sociology preyed on my religious conviction even before I went to theological seminary. First I had to complete a Bachelor of Arts (Admission) degree.

Shortly after Sharpeville I went to Langa one Sunday morning with a group of senior theology students to do missionary work. The stupidity of it all still amazes me. Two days before we went, residents had thrown stones at passing motorists and *Die Burger* had published a photo of two bloodied nurses sitting in their car which had a broken windscreen. But in we went, singing songs of praise and totally unaware of the political tensions of the situation.

Deep in the township, after we had parked our cars outside, I listened to a senior theology student trying to convince a group of residents of God's grace and, as a bonus, of the good work the government was doing for them. Soon we were surrounded by about a hundred people who made no secret of their resentment towards us. Softly I suggested to the preacher that it did not seem the Word was going to have much impact that day and that we should perhaps slowly start moving in the direction of the cars. This was the first time he noticed that trouble was brewing. With pale faces we started walking back to the cars. The crowd pelted us with pebbles and booed as we left; every now and then one of them tripped us up. Two blocks away from the cars, they frog-marched the professor of missionary science, the dignified and honourable Willie van der Merwe, out of a side street together with a few more students. By the time we got into our cars there must have been at least two hundred people, all screaming and swearing. Our car became stuck in the sand and the spinning wheels sent the dust flying. We got out to push and the crowd laughed and jeered at us. Finally we were on solid ground, and we drove in a deathly silence and with dusty faces back to Stellenbosch. That was the last time I undertook missionary work. Instead I began to read, philosophise and debate.

These pursuits have been a constant characteristic of my relationship with Rocky (Jannie) Gagiano. He was also at Wilgenhof, which is where our lifelong friendship began – thirty-eight years of philosophising and debating. Gagiano was supposed to study law, but he deceived both his father and the bursary donors by studying philosophy full time. Later he became a lecturer in political science. Through him I came to know the philosopher Johann Degenaar. Degenaar was on the theological seminary's list of undesirables and was, in the early 1960s, occupying himself with existentialism: Albert Camus, Jean-Paul Sartre, Martin Heidegger, Gabriel Marcel, Søren Kierkegaard, Friedrich Nietzsche, and so forth. In theology, Degenaar discussed the works of Bishop Robinson and Van Buren (the 'God is dead' theologians), and Teilhard de Chardin. Gagiano was not shy about his unbelief and doubt, and he drew me into countless religious debates.

In the Catholic priory there were young priests with whom a few of us held regular debates. One of the themes was the peripheral and central values of Catholicism. For example: was the Virgin Mary peripheral or central? Four of the five priests later left the priesthood and married. Only one, Father Albert Nolan, remained, and he became a liberation theologian. For me it was a time of intense intellectual and emotional experience.

It was also a time of increasing sexual tension and discontent. I was twenty-one and still a virgin. The noose of congregational chastity, which was expected of regular church-goers, pulled tighter and tighter. Head, body and conscience were in conflict and pulled in opposite directions. Things were not made easier by my friendship with Gagiano either; his increasing involvement in existentialism and the cutting personal arguments resulting from that. It became easier and easier to find a profound philosophical basis to prove my restraint needless. The era of the body was also about to come into its own.

My decision not to become a minister was thus not sudden. It would be convenient to claim it was inspired by a feeling of aversion to the political order of the time, especially in view of my later involvement. But apart from the Sobukwe incident at Wits, the experience in Langa township and a few brief brushes with student politics, I was, politically speaking, relatively unaware. My decision was a cerebral one, based on religious considerations. Intellectually it no longer made sense to me and I simply no longer believed in God.

One late summer afternoon, when I told F.J.M. Potgieter, dean of the faculty and professor of dogmatics, at his home that I had decided to give up my theological studies, all I said was that I no longer felt the call. He had no argument to counter this; after all, it was not his job to call or uncall. He asked that we pray together and we knelt down in his study and he asked the Lord to save me for teaching.

He must have had a premonition. I was in my second year at the theological seminary and while I studied for the degree of Bachelor of Divinity, I took honours in sociology as an extra. I became more and more absorbed in sociology and when I got a good pass at the end of 1963,

I was offered a temporary junior lecturer's post. And so my career as an academic began. It was the beginning of an unrestricted assault on my intellect, which continues to this day.

Before I started lecturing, I had financed my term at university through a scholarship from the Helpmekaar Study Fund and three years of holiday work as a disinfecting officer for the Johannesburg municipality. A disinfecting officer disinfects rooms where people have died from contagious diseases. You mix formalin and water in a ratio of one-to-four in a large bucket, plug all the holes and crevices in the room with white glue and newspaper, pump until the bucket is empty and the room full, then quickly leave the room and seal the door as well. The next day you issue a certificate stating that the room is now suitable for normal use. Thus I disinfected servants' quarters, bedrooms, hospital wards and even a telephone booth in Soweto. A beggar had died in the booth after consuming too much methylated spirits. What this had to do with contagion is still a mystery. Nevertheless, my experiences as a disinfecting officer helped me to think a bit about justice in life.

My doctoral thesis was so esoteric that I am still the only person who can get excited about it. At that stage, the dominant analytical framework in sociology at Stellenbosch was the theory of Talcott Parsons of Harvard. His basic point of departure was that actions have to be understood in terms of the individual's interaction with a situation and that this situation can be divided analytically into four systems of action: physical, psychological, social and cultural. Based on this premise, he built a massive, highly complex analytical and conceptual framework, which took me at least three years to master. My problem, however, was that I had no way of judging the validity of Parsons's theory.

There was so much uncritical intellectual acclaim for his work that one constantly found the validity of the theory explained in terms of the theory itself. I would have to take up a position outside Parsons's framework if I were to decide on its acceptability. In this manner I ended up in the domain of the philosophy of science, which became a lifelong hobby and in which I never developed more than an elementary competence. At least it sharpened my feeling for tautological arguments and thus helped me solve the problem regarding Parsons. That, then, was the subject of my thesis: to develop an independent methodological position in order to evaluate the intellectual acceptability of Parsons's theory. And in this way I also arrived at the problem of teleological statements.

But first I surrendered myself for a while to existentialism, perhaps in reaction to the formalism of theology. It was fashionable to mention Sartre and Camus casually if one wished to sound profound, and to deal with one's personal sense of alienation by cultivating an alternative lifestyle as portrayed in the works of people like Jack Kerouac, Henry Miller, Lawrence Lipton and André Gors. Meaninglessness was the 'in' thing and one never became too excited about anything. The only measure of the genuine was the senses, and the pathos of everyday existence lay in nonrecurrence and transience. As Camus put it: the only meaningful question was why a person should not commit suicide. The only reliable knowledge was the immediacy of your own experience; nothing and no one else could tell you where to find meaning. But such relentless melancholy cannot be sustained for too long. Ultimately there is nothing that unique about one's own fear of dying. If through Parsons I discovered the untenability of tautological thinking, then existentialism taught me an aversion to solipsism and relativism. Both kindled my interest in the philosophy of science. My current dislike of postmodernism springs largely from my experience of existentialism – most postmodernist insights are in any event old hat.

I guess it was inevitable that my experiences at the theological seminary, Parsons's scholasticism, the philosophy of science, teleology and existentialism would put me in conflict with the ideology and policies of apartheid. Apartheid was a civic religion with an essentially teleological and, therefore, tautological logic of explanation, which also fundamentally impacted on the daily lives of the majority of South African citizens. In short, it was a moral and intellectual embarrassment and an insult. Put differently: apartheid told you what the role of history was, what your place and role in it were and that you, personally, could do nothing about it. But those in power coincidentally enjoyed all the privileges and it was their 'historical duty' to 'lead' all other excluded groups towards 'maturity and wisdom'.

I began to develop a deep revulsion and contempt for the ruling regime, especially its moral complacency and hypocrisy. The problem was, however, that I felt just as uncomfortable with the dominant liberation ideology of the day, namely communism with its Marxist methodology. Karl Popper in particular – through his works *The Open Society and Its Enemies* and *The Poverty of Historicism* – and one of his most distinguished students, Ernest Gellner, had a strong influence on me. To this day I have an almost generic mistrust of large-scale social engineering and the social prophets of liberation. We simply know too little about the factors that influence social reality to impose the doubtful benefit of our own ignorance on others – especially through policies that do not take into account the possibility that we may be wrong. It is better to avoid what you have learnt through experience cannot work than to imagine you have the solutions to all problems. Both apartheid and communism suffered from this form of hubris as far as I was concerned.

My opposition to apartheid was therefore not that of the activist who had an alternative ideological solution, but rather that of a sceptical citizen who distrusted any large-scale solution to social problems. The racial privileges that came to me as a result of apartheid made me feel guilty, however, and made me susceptible to a more active form of resistance. But my scepticism about 'the final answer' incurred the mistrust of both the powers that were and the liberators. To one I was a 'useful idiot' of Moscow, to the other a 'pawn of racial capitalism'. The one thing that is tolerated less and less in a politically polarising situation is independence of thought, action and conviction. But this I only experienced later.

For ten years I wandered from one university to another: Stellenbosch, Rhodes, Cape Town, Wits. I lectured and marked papers and began to focus particularly on problems of modernisation and its impact on South African society. In 1973 I became head of the department at Wits, with the assumption that I would receive funds for research, have more time available for research and have fewer lecturing hours. None of this materialised. I was thirty-three years old and all I could see was a long career of administrative academic housekeeping stretching out ahead of me.

B.J. Vorster announced a general election on 24 April 1974 and I was approached by both the United Party and the Progressive Party to stand as candidate. A career in Parliament was the last thing on my mind. The only political activities I had been involved in up to then had been the Study Project on Christianity in Apartheid Society

(SPROCAS) in 1969; the organisation of a conference between coloured leaders and white Afrikaans-speaking farmers, academics, ministers of religion and journalists in Elgin near Grabouw in 1970 (the National Party and *Die Burger* regarded the whole affair as 'highly subversive'); the establishment of Synthesis, a multiracial discussion group consisting of Mangosuthu Buthelezi, Japie Basson, member of Parliament for the United Party, Curnick Ndamase, member of the Transkei cabinet, Nic Olivier, professor in Bantu administration at Stellenbosch, Colin Eglin, leader of the Progressive Party, M.T. Moerane, editor of *The World*, Mohammed Mayet, an Indian doctor, Dick van der Ross, rector of the University of the Western Cape, and Lou van Oudenhove, a doctor in the Cape whose idea it had been. I was secretary of the group, which B.J. Vorster dismissed as a 'leftist Prog nest'. Synthesis still exists (in early 2000), with more than a hundred members; Vorster is long gone. All these things were extra-parliamentary and were regarded as subversive in the political climate of the time.

I had enormous appreciation for Helen Suzman's lonely struggle in Parliament against the madness of apartheid. When I heard she intended to retire if no one else won a seat for the Progs, in order to support her I agreed to keep the other parties busy in Rondebosch so that Eglin would stand a better chance in Sea Point. I was repeatedly assured that I did not have a snowball's hope of winning Rondebosch, as it was a safe United Party seat. Based on this assumption I became the candidate for the Progressive Party in the Rondebosch constituency, and at two o'clock on the morning of 25 April 1974 I was announced as the new member of Parliament for the area.

On election day a coup in Portugal signalled the end of colonial rule in Mozambique and Angola. B.J. Vorster was rather unperturbed about it all. But for P.W. Botha, who was then minister of defence, it was the beginning of the Total Onslaught.

2 The Last White Parliament

NOTHING COULD HAVE PREPARED ME for Parliament under apartheid. Seven of us won seats in 1974 for the Progressive Party, a small liberal-democratic party. Both the National Party (NP) and the official opposition, the United Party, reacted hysterically. One saw us as the thin edge of the *Rooi Gevaar* wedge; the other as the instrument that destroyed its chance of beating the NP at the polls. Both were entrenched in a world of political unreality, totally out of touch with developing political trends on the extra-parliamentary terrain. Not that we Progs were necessarily familiar with them, but Helen Suzman had broad contact with black groups that had experienced the pain of official legislation being applied, and she regularly visited Robben Island to converse with the political detainees there. Through her we began to learn about a world that occupied most of the government's time, but for which the state felt no accountability. The white Parliament's right of existence lay in working full time at excluding black South Africans from the government of the country. Increasingly, this resulted in ritualised madness.

I experienced this for the first time at the start of 1975 when I found myself in a small chapel in the black squatter township KTC on the Cape Flats. Bishop Matualenga was speaking to about two hundred squatters. He told them that I came from Parliament, that I was a good white man and that, maybe, I could help them. These were conservative rural people who had come to the city out of a desperate need to survive. I had to ask the government not to knock down their shacks and not to chase them away.

I felt a rage surging up inside me at the absurdity of their plight. In those days the authorities still distinguished between 'urban Bantus' and 'homeland Bantus'; the urban ones had to have permission to be there. The government had decided that the Western Cape was to be a 'preferential area' for coloured labour, therefore black people were not allowed to go there. Nowhere in the world has urbanisation been stopped. But here for the first time it would happen, using force and violence if necessary.

I said I would see what I could do. When I had finished speaking, a young man came to me and asked if I would go with him. He took me to his squatter hut and led me inside. On the wall was a certificate from the Metal Box company in recognition of fifteen years of meritorious service. The man explained that he had been living in the single quarters in Guguletu. One day, his wife from the Transkei pitched up with their three children and said she could no longer survive on the money he sent home. She said it was better for them to manage one household instead of two. She fell pregnant and gave birth to triplets. The birth paralysed her lower body and the man went to the Transkei where, according to tradition, he married a 'nurse' to look after his wife and six children. While he was telling me this, he pulled open a curtain and told his wife, who was sitting on the floor, to drag herself around so that she could show me she was paralysed. He pleaded with me to explain to the minister that he was not a crook and to ask the minister to leave them in peace so that they could try to survive to the best of their abilities. Just then an official from the department of Bantu administration arrived and said he was obliged to arrest me because I was in a black township without a permit. His name was Loxton.

I told him not to waste his time or mine and that he could serve a warrant on me at Parliament.

M.C. Botha, the minister of Bantu affairs, instructed Loxton to summons me to appear in the Wynberg District Court. I told my caucus that if the magistrate offered me the choice of a fine or a prison sentence, I would go to jail. I think my lawyer must have told the magistrate of my intention because he released me with a warning.

Andries Treurnicht was the deputy minister charged with these matters and I went to plead with him for this family. I appealed to his humanity; after all, he had been a *dominee* for a long time. Treurnicht assured me of his compassion but said the policy was crystal-clear and consistent: the 'nurse' and the six children had to go back to the Transkei, the wife to a clinic (where, for God's sake?) and the man back to the single quarters in Guguletu. (This is the same Treurnicht who allowed the school uprisings to explode on 16 June 1976 with the government's crystal-clear and consistent policy on language in black schools. Twenty-three years later, on the same day, Thabo Mbeki was sworn in as the second democratically elected president of South Africa.)

Back in Parliament we debated the amendment to the Prevention of Illegal Squatting Act, which made specific provision for the destruction of, among others, the very shacks I had visited. Fanie Potgieter, member of Parliament for Port Elizabeth North, said it was high time that the people of the Transkei who came to 'bask in the Western Cape sun like a bunch of lizards' returned to where they had come from. In my response I suggested to him that if his brain were dynamite, it would not be strong enough to blow the spectacles off his nose. The speaker called me to order and I had to apologise. (This is one of the expressions I remember from my father. He always used it to refer to himself. The other was: 'It's so stuffy, you'd have to fart to get fresh air.' Not a bad description of Parliament.)

This incident happened right at the beginning of my parliamentary career, but the feeling of absurdity and unreality it provoked in me never left me as long as I remained there. It astounded me that apparently intelligent people could utter such intellectual rubbish with passion and piety. I would sit there, watching them, and would say to myself, 'You can't honestly believe what you're saying.' (When we came to the 'new South Africa', a few of them indeed admitted to me that they never really believed their own arguments and that they had known I had been right in many of the things I said.) The only rational explanation I could find was that, once you are a state employee and a lackey of those in power, it is not difficult to lose your capacity for sound judgement. I honestly believe there are habitual bootlickers; they cannot help themselves. They were lackeys of the old establishment and now they are equally keen lackeys of the new one. The same passion with which they offered advice to the Broederbond, B.J. Vorster and P.W. Botha is now available for Thabo Mbeki and the new guys. I think it has to do with the temptations of power and a deep-seated need to be part of the current establishment. F.W. de Klerk's autobiography, *The Last Trek*, epitomises this phenomenon. He was easily one of the most skilful defenders of apartheid, and was always pushed forward in debates where, in a scholastic and eloquent manner, apparent sense had to made out of nonsense. With a crooked, cynical smile on his face he defended the moral and practical justification of Bantu education, group areas, separate amenities, the temporary status of black people without South African citizenship in urban areas, and even the Tricameral Parliament (despite the fact that he had personally informed me in the lobby it would not work). But of one thing he never lost sight: he wanted to become the chief state official and for this, everything was possible and nothing essential.

In 1979 I became leader of the official opposition in the Assembly, more or less at the same time as P.W. Botha became prime minister. He succeeded Vorster. For as long as I was in Parliament during Vorster's term as prime minister, he did not once greet me or acknowledge my existence. I must have been the ultimate *hendsopper* or *hanskakie* in his eyes. (After the 1999 elections, Harald Pakendorf told me in passing, 'In your time you were the leader of a party and an Afrikaner for whom all the Jews voted. Now a Jew is leader of a party that succeeded yours and most Afrikaners vote for him.' I wonder what Vorster would have thought of this.)

In the 1981 election we increased our number of seats from seven to twenty-seven. In the meantime, Andries Treurnicht had broken away from the NP to form the Conservative Party (CP). The CP had a few seats less than we had and we started dreaming of a parliament that would be ungovernable because the NP could be outvoted on important issues through a combined opposition. For example, both the CP and ourselves were opposed to the creation of a tricameral parliament: they because coloureds and Indians would be included and we because blacks would be excluded.

The night after the results of the 1981 elections I awoke to a blazing fire in my study. The previous evening we had stayed up right through the night awaiting the results and my children had slept in the study. Mercifully, on the night of the fire they were back in their own bedrooms. The flames were so bad that there was literally nothing left of my library. The firemen told me that the fire could only have been caused by arson. To this day I do not know how it happened, although I have my suspicions. In the parliamentary lobby I was told that the security police was spreading the rumour that my young son had started the fire.

The public's reaction was overwhelming. Crates of books were sent to me and I soon had a bigger library than my old one. The only problem was that I was not interested in ninety per cent of the books I received, and nothing can replace one's own annotations, lecture notes or writings. I suppose the animosity towards me and the Progressive Federal Party (PFP) had increased because we had performed so well in the election. Shortly thereafter the threatening calls began and my car tyres were slashed a number of times.

The process of creating the tricameral legislation was a lesson and a demonstration of constitutional cynicism at its best. With pomp and ceremony Botha announced the establishment of the constitutional commission to investigate the formulation of a new constitution for South Africa in which all its inhabitants, including 'urban blacks', would enjoy meaningful political rights. I also served on the commission and we travelled across the country to collect so-called testimony. The outcome of it all was that coloured and Indian minorities were pulled into central government in a situation of co-optive dominance; blacks were finally stripped of citizenship and 'urban black people' could obtain self-rule at local government level. Jac Rabie of the coloured Labour Party said to me at the time, 'They are bringing us closer to power to show us how far away from it we will remain.' He later joined the NP.

A referendum was called for whites to decide on the acceptability of this new constitution. It was during participation in the referendum campaign that I began to realise that I was wasting my time in Parliament. The government sold the whole process as 'a step in the right direction', and it was absolutely astonishing who and how many swallowed this. Even Franklin Sonn, an ambassador to the United States in the new South Africa, actively campaigned to persuade whites to vote 'yes'. He was also instrumental in persuading the Reverend Allan Hendrickse and David Curry of the Labour Party to participate in the new Parliament. One morning, in front of St George's Cathedral in Wale Street, I asked Franklin, 'What on earth has got into you?' He laughed from deep down and said, 'Tomorrow, when I'm in Paradise, I'll think of you.' (In 1987 Franklin came with us to Dakar and emotionally begged for forgiveness from the African National Congress. He later received his reward.)

Andries Treurnicht and I lost hopelessly in the 1983 referendum – for precisely the opposite reasons. The traditional support of the Progs deserted us *en route* to a 'step in the right direction' and all the enlightened Afrikaners who now sit so cosily with the ANC worked their fingers to the bone for the yes vote. My first reaction was that we should withdraw from Parliament and I discussed this with the leadership. Helen Suzman and Colin Eglin, in particular, were opposed to such a move and after hours of debate they persuaded me to stay on for another year. I lasted another three years. During this period, mass protest action against the Tricameral Parliament and the so-called Koornhof Laws – which gave 'urban blacks' limited government functions as consolation for their exclusion from the country's central government – started making the townships ungovernable. Indeed, ritualised madness. One had only to spend an afternoon in the Tricameral Parliament to experience this first-hand.

For twelve years I tried to break down apartheid from an

opposition stance in white politics. My resignation in 1986 was the best commentary I could offer on my attempts. Parliament as an institution was increasingly rendered powerless through two conflicting, polarising political tendencies: the extra-parliamentary struggle for the freedom of the ANC and the Total Strategy of an increasingly military autocracy under the leadership of P.W. Botha. The PFP was eventually reduced to a powerless spectator, a well-meaning decoration of parliamentary pretence. We were overwhelmed by the contradictions of our position. While we emphasised the need for negotiation politics on every occasion, the unfurling political conflict was a daily negation of our attempts.

Botha and his colleagues treated Parliament with thinly disguised contempt and, with the eager co-operation of the security forces, they manipulated, lied to and misled it.

One day, Pik Botha told me he would like to speak to me confidentially in his office. As minister of foreign affairs he wanted to know whether I as leader of the opposition would help to make Crossroads – a squatter area on the edge of urban Cape Town to which rural black people were streaming – less of an international embarrassment and focus. Since black people were not supposed to be there and because the Western Cape was the 'preferential area' for coloureds, the authorities regularly targeted Crossroads, bulldozing the shacks in an attempt to force the people to return to the rural areas from where they had come. Every such effort was a lazy journalist's dream; they flocked in great numbers to the raids on Crossroads.

The solution was obvious, I told Botha: recognise the rights of these people to permanent residence and the problem solves itself. No, Botha said, it was not that simple and, besides, the security forces were increasingly regarding such areas as security risks. I then made it clear that I had no respect for nor confidence in Adriaan Vlok or Magnus Malan, respectively minister of police and minister of defence, and that both had misled me and lied to me in my official capacity. At that time they denied we were destabilising Mozambique even though the whole world knew it.

About a week later, Pik again asked to see me 'confidentially' because, he said, he wanted me to meet a 'sensitive' foreign visitor. When I arrived at his office, only Pik and Malan were present. Pik then told Magnus that I did not trust him; that I was convinced that South Africa was destabilising Mozambique despite the Nkomati Accord (the agreement of peaceful coexistence, which had been signed by P.W. Botha and Samora Machel a few months earlier). Malan swore by all that is holy that this was not the case. Pik then suggested that Malan persuade a group of farmers from Nelspruit to plough some land for Machel as a gesture of goodwill, and that he use this as a pretext under which to 'clean up' Renamo, the rebel movement in Mozambique, 'right up to the north'. Malan pretended to consider the suggestion seriously, but after some 'reflection' he said he could not allow his men to be shot at while they were protecting the farmers. They really thought they were fooling me.

Just then Jonas Savimbi walked in, accompanied by Brand Fourie, director-general of foreign affairs, and some others from Savimbi's entourage. With great expressions of gratitude to the South African government Savimbi began to explain how the war in Angola was progressing. He was full of confidence that Luanda would 'soon fall'. Just after Savimbi left I told Pik that if he thought he could compromise my resistance to South Africa's destabilisation of neighbouring countries in this manner, he was mistaken.

Shortly thereafter, in the middle of 1985, Colin Eglin, chairman of the PFP, and I went on a tour to Australia and New Zealand. During our journey I said to him that I thought we were wasting our time in Parliament; that if we could not come up with an imaginative strategy we should leave. He suggested that we both work on such a strategy and since it was the end of the year, that we discuss it in the new year. From the office of Bob Hawke, then prime minister of Australia, I phoned P.W. Botha's office and requested a meeting as soon as I arrived back in South Africa. Eglin and I had decided to try once more to convince P.W. to unban the ANC, free Nelson Mandela and start negotiations.

I went to Canada before returning home. Grey with exhaustion after the long flight I went directly from the airport to P.W.'s offices in the Union Buildings. I literally pleaded with him and said that if he wanted to 'pull the teeth' of the ANC's armed struggle, he should release Mandela and start negotiating. (This tooth-pulling story later upset some ANC members; I had been unaware that P.W. was taping our conversation and that later, after my resignation, he would release it to embarrass me. The armed struggle's teeth were pulled in precisely this manner when F.W. de Klerk made his speech in Parliament on 2 February 1990.) P.W. just licked his lips and, with a crooked smile, said that I did not realise that the majority of black people actually supported him. This was, perhaps, the moment when I finally decided to resign.

At about the same time I read in a newspaper that the diary of a certain Colonel Vass of Renamo had been confiscated in northern Mozambique. In it he provided a detailed account of how Renamo and the South African Army had destabilised Mozambique before, during and after the signing of the Nkomati Accord. I compared some of the dates in the diary with my own and saw that they corresponded with the time when Pik and Malan had tried to sell me the Nelspruit farmers story. I made enquiries at the top structures of the defence force and they informed me that this was communist propaganda.

In December 1985, while on holiday in Swaziland, I worked on the strategy Eglin and I had discussed in Australia. Briefly what it came down to was that I proposed that the PFP resign from all twenty-seven seats, thereby forcing by-elections; that those among us who won refused to take up their seats unless the government revoked the Population Registration Act. (This was the generic law that paved the way for all other apartheid legislation; when it was tabled for the first time, it was called the 'Magna Carta of race relations'.) My strategy was intended to create some form of constitutional or political crisis.

But while I was working on the strategy, I wondered if there was a way of getting to the truth about Colonel Vass's diaries. I phoned Samora Machel's office in Maputo and asked whether I could visit him. He replied, 'Come as soon as you can.'

It cost me R800 to hire a single-engine plane. At the airport in Maputo, the minister of security, Sergio Vierra, welcomed my eighty-year-old father-in-law and me. In a government house near the Polana Hotel, Vierra went systematically through the diary of Colonel Vass with us. He told us that he had done the same thing a few weeks earlier with Pik Botha, who went pale with fright and immediately called Niel Barnard of National Intelligence to request protection for himself as soon as he returned to the Waterkloof air force base. According to Vierra, Pik was convinced that his own people wanted to do him in because he was in possession of too much classified information.

Sergio Vierra is a classicist who enjoys reading Latin and Greek, and writing poetry. He is also a hard-line revolutionary, who has suffered enormous personal hardship. Late that night, after enjoying red wine and cognac, we drove through the slums of Maputo in his official vehicle and I asked him if he had ever tortured anyone. He started crying softly and said yes, but none of it made any difference. We both became despondent at the thought of the children who had lost eyes, legs and arms through the senselessness of war.

The next morning Machel strode up and down in front of me in his office. 'What is Botha trying to do? I can't make war against him. He knows this. Why is he destroying my country? He's only creating problems for his own country. Tell him that, just as Hitler's war ended in Berlin, so his shall end in Pretoria. But how many people does he want to kill before that happens?'

Back in Swaziland I phoned Pik Botha's offices and requested a meeting as early as possible in the new year. Pik was his predictable garrulous self. As he had done so many times before, he tried to defend the indefensible as if what he was doing was acceptable. I was none the wiser for the meeting.

After I had consulted Harry Oppenheimer, Zach de Beer, Colin Eglin, Nic Olivier, Helen Suzman, Andrew Savage, Errol Moorcroft, Pierre Cronjé and Peter Gastrow – the members of my caucus I trusted most – I realised that my strategy held no appeal. (I was convinced that one or two other members spoke directly to P.W. Botha and therefore did not want to discuss my plan too soon in front of the whole caucus.) Eglin had no plan other than to struggle on. Not one of them believed that I was serious about resigning, even though I repeatedly told them I would do so.

I wrestled with how long I should wait before informing

the rest of the caucus or party of my decision to resign. If I did it too early, both the party and I would find ourselves in a politically untenable position. Consequently, half an hour before I was due to respond in the no-confidence debate, I informed the caucus that I would announce my resignation to Parliament that afternoon. Their bewilderment and indignation knew no bounds – understandably.

P.W. Botha started the session by grilling Pik Botha for suggesting that South Africa could one day have a black president. By the time Botha sat down, Pik was practically hiding under his front bench.

The general expectation was that I would concentrate solely on this issue in my reply. I totally ignored it and began motivating why I considered further participation in Parliament a waste of time. A deathly silence descended – total surprise in NP ranks and confusion around me.

When I sat down, Hendrik Schoeman, leader of the Assembly, jumped up, totally perplexed, and asked if I would come back on the following Monday so that the Assembly could take proper leave of me. P.W. was completely dumbfounded. He walked over, shook my hand and said, 'Thank you for your civility.'

In the course of the weekend Eglin phoned me and said that the caucus would find it a 'sick-making' experience if I were to go back to Parliament on the Monday. I should rather stay away.

That Monday, my secretary Jenny Nothard and I packed my books and left. It was one of the most liberating experiences of my life when I walked away from the last white Parliament. But it was also painful, for me and for others.

3 Relationships and Coincidences

I MET BREYTEN BREYTENBACH for the first time at a University of Cape Town summer school, where we both participated in a series of lectures on the Sestigers, the Afrikaans literary movement of the 1960s. As so many others, this event was also organised by the late Jim Polley – former Methodist minister, later the organiser of film festivals and nonstop entertainment, and an untamed adolescent to the end. On the evening of Breyten's formal address, Schalk Pienaar – a tormented but devoted member of the Afrikaner establishment – sat weeping at the press table as Breyten likened his role in relation to Afrikaans to that of the guide in the Cedarberg, who spent the night next to the corpse of his wife to prevent the leopard from devouring her. He said Afrikaans was becoming a language for epitaphs. He subsequently tried to launch Okhela and, before I could blink, I was in Parliament and he in prison.

The next time Breyten and I met was when I visited him in jail. This also happened through a coincidence.

One day, I received a pile of anonymous documents on my desk at Parliament. This was in 1979, shortly after I had become leader of the official opposition and P.W. Botha prime minister. The anonymous letter that accompanied the documents stated that they came directly from the department of mineral and energy affairs. It claimed that the documents offered proof of massive corruption in the oil trade and said P.W. Botha had received the same set of documents.

I thought it would be preferable for P.W. and me to tackle a problem of this magnitude together. That afternoon I wrote him a note in the Assembly, which I sent over by messenger and in which I rather politely and diffidently requested a meeting to discuss the matter. P.W. read the note, crumpled it up, stuck it in his pocket and walked out. Half an hour later, the messenger told me there was a telephone call for me. Commodore Ehlers, P.W.'s *aide de camp*, said, 'Doctor, the boss is very angry.' I asked him why and he replied that it would be better if I spoke to him myself. P.W. came on the line and said, 'Who the **** do you think you are, sending me a note without putting it in an envelope?' I was dumbstruck. I replied, 'Man, if you're so keen on envelopes, I'll go and buy you a dozen right now and send them to you,' and I put the phone down. For about four weeks P.W. did not speak to me and refused to acknowledge me. (According to parliamentary tradition, the prime minister acknowledges the leader of the opposition with a nod at the opening of proceedings each day, prior to the formal prayers led by the speaker.) We sat directly opposite each other in the Assembly, but he consistently avoided eye contact.

One Wednesday evening, I was listening to Sporie van Rensburg of Rosettenville, who was participating in the railways debate. He spoke beautiful Afrikaans. Suddenly, P.W. leaned forward and said to me, 'Afrikaans is a beautiful language, isn't it?' I said it was, and that I would really like to come and see him about Afrikaans. He said I should arrange an appointment. Commodore Ehlers told me I could come in a week's time. I had, in the meantime, been nagging first Louis le Grange, minister of police, and later his successor, Kobie Coetsee, to be allowed to visit Breyten in Pollsmoor. After many months, I was granted permission.

Breyten was sitting next to a warden. I asked him what I could do to help. He said he would preferably want to be released but until that happened, he would like a contact visit with Yolande. The following day I told P.W. I would appreciate his help in getting one of the masters of the Afrikaans language out of prison. He knew immediately to whom I was referring and pointed out that someone sentenced in terms of article 6 of the Anti-terrorism Act could not qualify for parole. I responded by saying that those who made the law could also change it. With a characteristic licking of his lips and crooked smile he said he would discuss it with Kobie. I added that Breyten would like a contact visit with Yolande. 'What is that?' P.W. asked, immediately suspicious. I explained that for the previous five years, Breyten had only been able to speak to Yolande through a glass window and that he wished to speak to her face to face, in the presence of a prison guard. I think P.W. was genuinely shocked when he asked, 'Do you mean that up to now they haven't been able to do that?' But Breyten still did not get the contact visit.

The second time I visited Breyten in prison, I had to do so under the pretext of an official inspection, in the presence of the commissioner of prison services, a rather stout fellow with a thick neck. This pretext was necessary as it was felt that too many personal visits would create a precedent. First I visited the maternity ward, then the kitchen and finally the cells where prisoners stood on their 'taxis' (dishcloths to keep the floor shiny). One of them, his upper front teeth missing, waited while we inspected his cell. Brimming with joviality, the commissioner clapped his arm around the man's shoulders and asked, 'And what are you in here for, my friend?' The prisoner stuck his tongue in the gap left by his teeth and said, 'Thodomy, general.'

Two years later, article 6 was amended to allow for parole. Kidson was released first, then Breyten. It just goes to show what can happen when you fail to put a note into an envelope.

In October 1986 I received an invitation from France Liberté to attend an anti-apartheid cultural festival in Dakar, Senegal. This was Breyten's doing. France Liberté was Danielle Mitterrand's foundation, and he was in favour with her.

Earlier that year, in February, I had suddenly resigned as leader of the opposition in the National Assembly and I was in the process of setting up the Institute for a Democratic Alternative for South Africa (IDASA) along with Alex Boraine – who had resigned in equally dramatic fashion shortly after me. We were not quite sure what to do with our lives right then and thought that such an institute could offer some excitement under the prevailing circumstances.

Boraine and I realised that, if we were to set up an impartial institute like IDASA, we would need to win the support of strategic groups and individuals in both camps, namely the 'system' and the 'struggle'. The situation was rapidly becoming polarised and neutral organisations found themselves gripped in a merciless vice: you belonged to either one side or the other.

Towards the end of my parliamentary career, I had led the executive committee of the Progressive Federal Party to Lusaka, Zambia, to meet with the leadership of the ANC. It was a turning point for me. Nothing brought home the isolation and insulation of Parliament more than my first meetings with Thabo Mbeki, Alfred Nzo, Mac Maharaj and Oliver Tambo. There could be no resolution of the conflict without ANC participation.

Approving noises were made in Lusaka about our resignations and the general assumption was that we would immediately join the ANC. No one expected us to establish an independent institute to promote dialogue. When we tested the waters with Mbeki, he said that we should see if we could obtain the support of the internal struggle movement, in other words, the United Democratic Front or the Mass Democratic Movement.

Dogmatists on both sides of the conflict had scant enthusiasm for something like IDASA. To them, negotiation politics meant either stalling tactics which undermined the inevitable revolution, or 'sell-out' politics which would relinquish power to the communists. Raymond Suttner, one of the hard-line communists, put it to me bluntly that 'the people' had already decided what type of democracy they wanted and that it was not necessary to set up an institute for this purpose. Mbeki, on the other hand, was in favour of the idea, even if it was simply out of curiosity to see what such an institute could deliver.

Boraine and I both had to undergo a clandestine baptism of fire with the local struggle movement. A car fetched me from Port Elizabeth airport and, after we had changed vehicles several times, I found myself standing alone at ten o'clock at night in New Brighton township. The country was in the throes of a state of emergency, and Casspirs and other military vehicles patrolled the townships. Someone tapped me on the shoulder and told me to follow him. In a small tin shack, five young masked comrades sat waiting; they asked what IDASA was all about. They listened, then said that they would make contact again and took me back to my hotel. Clearly they must have communicated with Lusaka and/or Robben Island, because a few weeks later we received an answer: the struggle would co-operate with our efforts.

We had no money. Liberal American institutions like Rockefeller, Ford and Carnegie wanted nothing to do with us. We were too white, we were not foot soldiers of the struggle, or perhaps they were concerned that we would threaten their existing projects. Björne Lindström, Norwegian *chargé d'affaires*, believed in us and gave us money to go on a begging mission. We would not, in any case, get any money from inside South Africa. In the beginning, the Friedrich Naumann Stiftung of Germany's Freie Demokratische Partei (FDP) helped us, as did the Swedes, Norwegians and Danes, but it was tough. We started to arrange small meetings to promote interactive communication, especially between white and black youths. We also arranged so-called 'township tours', during which visitors could enjoy a meal and conversation at the homes of local residents. The interest was overwhelming and we could not keep up with the demand. Once again the levels of ignorance, isolation and prejudice were staggering. Alex and I worked for no pay; money was too scarce. It was only much later, as executive director of IDASA, that he could draw his first salary. I was never an employee.

It was then that I received the invitation from France Liberté to go to the island of Gorée. It was probably your average anti-apartheid conference: angry speeches, pious resolutions and plenty of time to have fun. The conference was held on the mainland, but the concert was on the island. After listening to Miriam Makeba and other artists, Breyten and I sprawled under a baobab tree and chatted. A young, seriously inebriated Senegalese fellow told us he admired us 'white Boers' for daring to take a stand against apartheid outside our country, in Africa. He was convinced our lives would be in danger when we returned, and offered to teach us a secret phrase that would protect us against all evil and danger. Just then, Nthato Motlana joined us, full of excitement. 'They tell us at home that we blacks don't know how to trade or manage a business. Have you seen the market here? I've walked past hundreds of stalls and couldn't believe my eyes. I told myself, there must be a coolie somewhere who owns the whole lot.' While Motlana spoke, the young Senegalese disappeared in search of another thirst-quencher. (Breyten and I have been living in fear of our lives ever since.) Motlana was later to be chairman of IDASA's board for several years.

Breyten and I talked about how we could get a group of Afrikaners to come and speak to the ANC leadership in Dakar, but more especially on Gorée. The situation at home was so bogged down that such an event could act as a release mechanism. 'Create the facts,' he said, 'and work with the consequences.' We fired each other up with the possibilities: he would, with the help of Danielle Mitterrand, take care of protocol and liaise with President Abdou Diouf of Senegal; Alex and I had to take care of the finances, the Afrikaners and the executive members of the ANC. We did not have a clue how much it would cost, whether the Afrikaners and the ANC would come, or whether P.W. Botha would prevent it. But by that stage of the evening, no price was too high and no sacrifice too great. The symbolism of Gorée as the heart of the slave trade in the old days did not escape us either. *'Hier kom 'n ding.'* (Breyten's most menacing expression.)

And so Boraine and I found ourselves once again on a begging mission, this time to the United States of America. We had worked out that we would need about R400 000. From Carnegie, Ford and Rockefeller we again came away empty-handed. Despondent and depressed we walked around Washington. The National Endowment for Democracy, a bi-partisan organisation of the American Congress, said it liked our project, but doubted whether Congress would approve it since Jessie Helms would veto any dialogue with 'communists'! One of its directors said he knew of a rather eccentric billionaire in New York who might be interested, since he had previously been involved with South Africa. We wondered whether he would see us at such short notice. They made a phone call and ten minutes later we were told that the man would see us the following day, Saturday, over lunch at his apartment in Manhattan. His name was George Soros.

We knew nothing about him. Testing the waters, we talked about this and that: the current situation in South Africa, his previous association with the University of Cape Town and his subsequent disappointment with that experience, his involvement in Eastern Europe and his attempts to strike a blow against communism there. He predicted that the Soviet Union would implode and that the face of Eastern Europe would change (that was in 1986). I asked him where his optimism stemmed from, and he said they were all 'closed' communities; that they were cutting themselves off ideologically from critical analysis and that, consequently, they would not be able to keep up with modern life; that the tension between ideology and reality would reach breaking point, and it would become increasingly impossible to fulfil the aspirations of ordinary people; that the whole system would collapse. I told him that we too came from a 'closed' community, and that it was precisely our intention to initiate projects that would challenge this; that the opposite of a 'closed' society was an 'open' one, and was he familiar with the works of Karl Popper who had made this idea the central theme of his book *The Open Society and Its Enemies?* It was like opening the floodgates.

As a seventeen-year-old, Soros, a Hungarian Jew, had fled to England from his motherland to escape death at the hands of the Nazis. At the London School of Economics he studied under Popper himself, and was persuaded by

Popper's views based on the philosophy of science, namely that human knowledge and insight can never be perfect and that, because of this limitation, all statements had to be subjected to critical analysis; that knowledge and insight increased when ignorance and errors were acknowledged; that societies which supported these principles made greater progress and were more adaptable in times of change; and so forth. After a few years of doing odd jobs, Soros established an investment fund with some family money and departed with £10 000 for the United States, where he managed Quantum Investment and Asset Management Fund. In the course of time, it became the most successful investment company of any one individual in the twentieth century and made Soros an extremely wealthy man. So wealthy that he decided to literally give away a part of his wealth to promote Popper's central idea of an 'open' society. This has meant that most of his philanthropic work has taken place in 'closed' societies, including the country of his birth, Hungary – then still under communist rule.

As we listened to the numerous projects Soros supported through his Open Society Foundations in Central and Eastern Europe, I was struck by the remarkable combination of idealism, pragmatism and scepticism in the man. Soros is definitely not a fragile soul who, overwhelmed by feelings of guilt about his wealth, supports philanthropic initiatives in order to gain social recognition. He does not attempt to hide his pride in his financial success but he is also sharply self-critical, and admits with equal candour both the successes and failures of his philanthropic endeavours. It is the most intellectually considered handing out of money that I have ever encountered.

Conversation ranged far and wide over lunch and coffee. Every now and then Boraine cleared his throat to remind me why we were actually there. Soros saw this and said,

'I suppose you're looking for money. How much?' We explained the project to him and said we needed about US$150 000. He said he thought our country was doomed under the current regime, but that ours sounded like a worthwhile project to him. Then he signed a cheque for US$75 000 and wished us good luck.

In the lift, Boraine and I passed the cheque to and fro in disbelief. Soros did not ask for any guarantee and said, in passing, that we could send him a report if we wished. The only basis for his generosity had been our, at times, highly abstract conversation, and our shared admiration for the works of Karl Popper. We obtained the rest of the money from the ever-reliable Scandinavians and the Naumann Stiftung.

Anthony Sampson, in his official biography of Mandela, claims that the National Intelligence Service (NIS) had 'discreetly' supported the Dakar conference. That is the first I have heard of such support. Right at the beginning of his career with NIS, Niel Barnard, the head of the service, made it very clear to me in a presentation that the government of the day regarded even the role of my party in Parliament as part of the Total Onslaught. Never before, during or after the Dakar conference did he or any of his officials directly or indirectly reveal that they had supported the Dakar conference in any way, either discreetly or indiscreetly.

The Dakar conference came and went, and attracted considerable attention, internationally and especially locally. P.W. was fuming with rage, to put it mildly, along with quite a few white South Africans. Still, I think Dakar contributed to undermining a few defunct paradigms: it demystified the ANC, put paid to most of the stereotypes with which the South African regime had labelled it, and legitimised dialogue with the organisation. It also did away with some prejudices held by the ANC about Afrikaners, especially those of the monolithic, obtuse, pap-and-wors, bully-of-the-Bushveld variety.

Dakar was IDASA's magical moment as a nongovernmental organisation (NGO). From then on there was no shortage of funding. Even the previously cautious American institutions suddenly saw merit in the attempts of a few pale South Africans to challenge the political stalemate in South Africa. Lufthansa gave us one hundred economy-class tickets, valid for three years, to any of its international destinations.

After Dakar, we organised more conferences abroad between the ANC and people from 'inside' – in Leverkusen and Frankfurt, Germany; in Marly-le-Roi, France; in Lusaka, Zambia; in Harare and at the Victoria Falls, Zimbabwe. Alex and I were invited by the Chinese government to visit Beijing and Tianjing. Discussions focused on future constitutional structures for South Africa, economic and foreign policy, art, culture and the self-determination of minorities. Delegations from 'inside' consisted of economists, business people, lawyers, academics, journalists, artists, writers and even a few ministers of religion of different denominations. Within South Africa, similar projects began to take root. Co-operation with the ANC and other struggle organisations was no longer a problem, and a broad spectrum of non-struggle interest groups began to participate.

We also experienced heightened interest from official sources: shots were fired through our office windows, car tyres were slashed, anonymous threatening letters and calls were received, and two of our black co-workers were murdered – one of them definitely by the former Ciskei police force. Later, through Alex's participation in the Truth and Reconciliation Commission (TRC), we discovered that we were both recorded in the minutes of the State Security Council as 'politically sensitive persons'.

I was never involved in IDASA on a full-time executive basis but I assisted Boraine voluntarily. His life was almost completely taken up by IDASA, until formal negotiations between the ANC and the NP government started in 1990, following Mandela's unconditional release and the unbanning of the ANC. After the 1994 elections, in which the ANC received the majority vote and established a government of national unity with the NP and Inkatha, Alex became vice-president of the TRC.

In the meantime, I turned to business and lectured at a number of universities, primarily as a visiting professor at Wits Business School. Dakar left me with a strong sense of my destiny being bound to Africa and of how little I knew of the rest of the continent. The coincidence of my birth, specifically here in Africa, and the inevitability of my death have always been a source of endless self-exploration. One cannot choose where one is born, but to a limited degree, one can choose where one wants to die, and what one gets involved in and how one does so, before this occurs. Dakar helped me decide that I would meet my end here, in Africa.

Shortly after the Dakar conference, Breyten said we should go to Senegal again, if only to thank President Diouf for his support. With Lufthansa's help, plane tickets were not a problem. Diouf is to this day convinced that he, Breyten and I, on our own, pulled South Africa out of the quagmire. While Breyten and I were holding a postmortem of the conference in his office, Diouf suddenly said, 'Are you going to ignore all of us in the rest of Africa now that you have had your congress?' We were taken aback and did not know how to respond. We promised him there and then that we would come up with a plan.

That evening, at the home of a Senegalese lawyer, Benoit Ngom, who had helped us with arrangements for Dakar, Breyten and I began to whip each other up again. As we plundered the fruits of North African vines, visions swam through our minds: what was necessary was to get dialogue going between South Africa and the rest of the continent, on democracy, culture and development. Among ordinary people, so that we could reflect upon our mutual problems. Think of the unbelievable cultural wealth and diversity of the continent, the exchange of knowledge and experience. Look at all the lessons we could learn from postcolonial failures. No price was too high, no sacrifice too great to create an institute right here on the slave island of Gorée. Just think of the symbolism: from slavery to liberation in Africa! Even before we had finished the meal, we christened it the Gorée Institute for Democracy, Development and Culture in Africa. '*Hier kom 'n ding.*'

Once again I found myself on a begging mission to Scandinavia. But this time it was tough. Everyone was still in love with IDASA and its fight against apartheid. Africa was just too much of an abstraction. I secured just enough to make a start. André Zaaiman, who worked for IDASA in Pretoria, said he was keen to start the Gorée Institute. My daughter, Tania, who was working in Senegal at the time and was fluent in French, said she too was eager to help. The two of them worked for six months without salaries to get the institute off the ground.

Zaaiman is, in any sense of the word, remarkable. When he arrived in Senegal he could not speak a word of French; eighteen months later he was fluent in both French and the local language, Wolof. He grew up in a conservative Afrikaans-speaking household; received a master's degree in political science from the University of the Orange Free

State in Bloemfontein; was an officer in the South African Army during his conscription period and saw action in Angola. He turned against conscription and joined the ANC's Umkhonto weSizwe. He smuggled Dirk Coetzee of Vlakplaas fame out of the country for the first time. When Zaaiman went to Dakar in 1989, he was totally exhausted from working for the struggle. The top structures of the ANC were not enamoured of either of us when he departed.

During the first year, André and Tania worked full time to attain diplomatic immunity for the institute and to establish an infrastructure. Immunity was important for our credibility and to demonstrate the goodwill of the Senegalese government. We did not want the institute to be seen as an extension of internal Senegalese politics. After a year we received our accreditation at an official ceremony. The institute had diplomatic status. I was chairman, Zaaiman was executive director and my daughter assistant. But we were totally broke.

Back in South Africa, I wrote to Soros. I had not heard from him since Dakar and had only sent him a report of income and expenses. That had been two years before. I wrote that if he thought Dakar had been a bit quixotic, he should brace himself for my next request. I explained what we wished to achieve with the Gorée Institute and said we were seeking US$50 000 to get started. A week later he apologised for not having responded sooner and said, 'I trust you; where should I send the money?' What can one say about something like this?

The Gorée Institute flourished after this. The German government restored the Maison de Sudan – a beautiful old house on the island – and said that if the Senegalese government agreed, we could have it. The government offered it to the institute on a ninety-nine-year lease. Tania and André rented a house on the island, but my daughter returned to South Africa shortly afterwards when her mother passed away. André continued on his own. It was incredibly hard work, but at least now there was money for more staff.

During another visit, André showed me a beautiful old house, which, he said, could help overcome the institute's struggle for survival. If we could obtain it, we could use the house to lodge some of our staff and visitors, and it would save considerably on costs. Soros gave me US$300 000 and we paid the house in cash. Five years later, when the institute had proved itself, Soros decided to support our projects to the tune of US$500 000 annually. He has also stayed at the institute for a few days.

André and Breyten met with equal success on their begging missions. By 1997, the Gorée Institute had a network of approximately a thousand voluntary organisations across Africa; our developmental courses are being used by the private sector and governments from Eritrea to the Cape Verde Islands; poets and writers come to complete their works in the house on the island; banned Nigerian opposition groups, led by the Nobel Peace laureate Wole Soyinka, held discussions there; there is a computer centre on the premises and lessons are offered to groups from different parts of neighbouring countries; the school on the island is the first computer-literate school in Senegal; many individuals and groups from South Africa have visited Gorée and it has been decided to establish a twinning relationship between Robben Island and Gorée.

Diouf's question and Benoit Ngom's dinner shortly thereafter had far-reaching and unexpected consequences. Breyten and I now cluck like mother hens about Gorée.

I was a visiting research fellow at All Souls College, Oxford, when F.W. de Klerk made his dramatic speech in the South African Parliament on 2 February 1990. Mandela would be released, the ANC unbanned, apartheid laws repealed and negotiations would commence. A day or so later I lunched with Mbeki and Aziz Pahad in London, and they were still stunned at the speed of events. In October the previous year, the Berlin Wall had fallen – a symbolic event, which had signalled the end of organised communism in Europe, and ultimately in the world. The two events were not entirely unrelated. When I met De Klerk in his Cape Town office at the end of February, I asked him what had motivated him to make the speech. He replied that it had to some extent been a spiritual shift away from apartheid and that he would have been crazy not to take advantage of the gap that the collapse of communism offered him. He was of the opinion that this would weaken the ANC's bargaining position, and that he could tackle them from a position of power. Both the country and his mind were in a melting-pot.

Out of the blue, Soros phoned me one evening from New York. He said he was considering establishing an Open Society Foundation in South Africa and asked if I would be chairman. I reminded him that he had told me at our first meeting that our country was doomed, so what was this? Well, he said, things now looked much more promising than in many Central and Eastern European countries where he was involved and, what was more, the Americans were sitting back and did not want to help these countries to become 'open' societies.

I met Soros at the arrivals hall at Jan Smuts Airport, and we drove to Zoo Lake Restaurant to plan the establishment of the Open Society Foundation of South Africa (OSFSA) over lunch. Four days later it was launched. Soros has since met with Mandela, as well as members of the OSFSA board. Michael Savage, then vice-rector of the University of Cape Town, became the first executive director. In November of that year, Soros took board members on a trip through Central and Eastern Europe to see how his other Open Society Foundations functioned. We visited Berlin, Budapest, Warsaw and Kiev.

The fundamental objective of Open Society Foundations is to support or initiate projects that enhance the individual's freedom of choice in society, and that enable individuals to exercise their choices with increased self-awareness and responsibility. Therefore, the focus was on literacy, general education, freedom of the press and freedom of speech, an independent judiciary, the emancipation of rural women in particular, small business development, democratic constitutional development, primary health education, and so forth. The general assumption was that the more these features of community life were supported and strengthened, the better equipped communities would be to adapt to change, and that overall levels of misery and suffering could therefore be reduced. Within the first three years of its existence, OSFSA donated more than R120 million to worthy projects in South Africa.

Like Zaaiman, Mike Savage is a remarkable human being: fiercely loyal, hard-working and scrupulously honest. He has managed to have the smallest ratio of administrative to project costs of all Soros's foundations. (Never more than six per cent.)

In addition, we also managed to establish a housing structure with Soros's help: the National Urban and Reconstruction Housing Agency (NURCHA). It aims to make loans and credit available to families earning less than R1 500 per month. Cedric de Beer, the executive director, is blessed with the same qualities as Savage and he has an exceptional knowledge of South Africa's housing problems. Soros regards NURCHA as one of his model projects and has donated R200 million towards it.

In March 1997, Soros again visited South Africa and asked me to help set up Open Society Foundations in nine Southern African countries: Namibia, Angola, Botswana, Swaziland, Lesotho, Mozambique, Malawi, Zambia and Zimbabwe. The regional body designated to co-ordinate this was the Open Society Initiative for Southern Africa (OSISA), which was officially launched by Soros on Gorée in February 1998.

The chance 1986 meeting with Soros in his Manhattan apartment had unforeseeable consequences for me; new relationships enriched my life and deepened my experience of Africa immeasurably. I have met extraordinary people from this continent and continue to do so – people with boundless courage, endless patience and perseverance, who do not have the luxury of writing Africa off from the comfort of their living-rooms. It is not difficult to become despondent. There is an overwhelming need for the benefits of scientific and technological advancement. I am humbled by the unsentimental devotion of these people. In retrospect, the best thing I ever did was to resign from the South African Parliament.

In financial and political circles, Soros is a controversial figure. He is painted as a merciless speculator who does not hesitate to destroy national currencies for his own profit; an insatiable megalomaniac. Central bank governors are petrified of the possible consequences of his speeches or investments.

I do not help Soros make money, I just help him to give it away philanthropically. In our personal discussions he has made it clear that there is a tension between what he calls the 'amoral' movement of finance capital and the moral commitment underpinning philanthropy. Personally,

I find this a difficult distinction to accept. One implication could be that in the pursuit of profit one could inadvertently or intentionally play a role in 'closing up' a society while philanthropically 'opening' it up. It is at the same time not unusual for the manner in which money is made and then given away philanthropically to appear strange or even paradoxical. Just think of the tobacco, alcohol or oil industries. The stereotype of the tough, amoral businessman who chases profit and then buys social acceptance through charity and good deeds is well known.

In South Africa we have the strange case of the De Beers Diamond Company. Since the early 1950s, and up to the demise of the Soviet Union, De Beers paid the government of the Soviet Union a substantial commission annually to maintain a monopoly over the international diamond market. Russian communist Vladimir Shubin, in his book about the relationship between Moscow and the ANC, points out that the direct association between De Beers and the Kremlin ended formally in 1963, but was continued from London through a front organisation. This front organisation, Standard Charter, was used by both Anglo and De Beers. In this way, De Beers could regulate the price of diamonds through the Central Selling Organisation (CSO). It is estimated that the commission paid by De Beers was the single largest annual private sector contribution to the Communist Party of the Soviet Union, given that this party was effectively the government of the day. One can be mischievous and say that, while Soros was trying to bring communism down, De Beers was indirectly helping to keep it alive! Even worse, the South African Communist Party (SACP) received financial and other support directly from the government of the Soviet Union. In a roundabout way one could therefore argue that, for a while, Oppenheimer helped to pay Joe Slovo's salary! During this period, Oppenheimer was also one of the largest and most appreciated donors of the party that I represented in Parliament. Nobody would deny that there were always irreconcilable differences between my party and the SACP, least of all the communists.

So far I have no reason to feel ambiguous or morally compromised about the manner in which Soros makes money or spends it, perhaps also because we discuss the subject so often. I have never received a cent from him for my personal use – whether in the form of a salary, gift or investment tip, so I have no need to ingratiate myself with him. We have argued and debated as intellectual equals from the day we met.

Soros's concern that an unfettered market economy wreak havoc in a globalised world and threaten the possibility of creating 'open' societies is genuine. He is convinced that, if we do not attempt to develop common values to guide and organise international relations, we will see a world in which the strong grow stronger at the expense of the weak. He finds it ironic that, with the closed nature of communist societies destroyed, the stronger and more 'open' countries are doing so little to help smaller and weaker countries grow and become more 'open'. In this recklessness and neglect he sees the breeding-ground for new intolerant ideologies, which could unlock a series of small-scale but destructive conflicts. But Soros is man enough to speak for himself, and he does so frequently.

Through my experiences with him, I have discovered how a chance meeting, and untested mutual trust, can form the basis of a relationship that knows no bounds in terms of surprises and possibilities. I am indeed privileged, because he has by no means been the only such one.

4 Birthmarks

ONE DAY IN THE EARLY 1980s I had to see P.W. Botha *pro forma* about salaries and pensions for members of Parliament. It was customary for this never to become the source of party-political conflict. Consequently, this was to be a very short meeting. (It seems this tradition is still alive.) Having exchanged a few pleasantries, I got up to leave, but P.W. said he wished to raise another important matter with me. I asked what it was and he replied, 'I am worried about Andries Treurnicht.' I enquired why and he said, 'He is giving Afrikaners like you and me a bad name.' This was the first time since my entry into politics that a prominent Nationalist accepted me as an Afrikaner. As leader of the Conservative Party (CP), Treurnicht's colleagues would have found it almost impossible to refer to me in unqualified terms as an Afrikaner. An 'over-enlightened', '*hendsopper*', '*kafferboetie* Afrikaner' maybe, but never simply an Afrikaner. A frontbencher in his party once said with relish – to the great delight of his colleagues in Parliament – that only two Slabberts had come to South Africa: the one died childless and the other married a black woman.

Shortly thereafter, a woman turned up at my office in Parliament. She wanted me to help her obtain an American visa. She worked for the South African Navy and I suggested to her that she might obtain it more easily through government channels than through the opposition. She said it was too risky because she had formed a relationship with a black American diplomat and that they were in love. In that case, I said, it would be even easier to work through him. No, she said, she was worried that it would cause a sensation. I asked what made her so special. She replied, 'I am Andries Treurnicht's daughter.' I said I would see what I could do.

At the time, Koos van der Merwe was chief whip for the CP and the two of us got on well. His face was pale as he listened to what I had to say. I told him it was not my style to conduct politics at a personal level, but he knew that if P.W. Botha came to hear of this, Treurnicht would be in for a thrashing. Koos asked me to do nothing and especially to say nothing; he would investigate. A week later he confirmed what I had told him and said I should leave the matter there. They would 'resolve it internally'. Just before Van der Merwe walked out of the door, he turned around and announced, 'Van Zyl, I just want to tell you: you are a white man.' To be called an Afrikaner and a white man in the space of one year, notably by the leader of the NP and the chief whip of the CP, had to indicate that serious changes were afoot in white politics. No wonder F.W. de Klerk handed over power a few years later.

Article 5.4 (c) of the old Population Registration Act contains three criteria for determining whether someone is a coloured or not: the person must look like a coloured, must be accepted by the community as coloured and his or her parents must be coloured. An entire race classification bureaucracy, with a court, was set up to enforce this law. For us in the opposition it was an annual ritual to ask the relevant minister, not without malice, how many people had been re-classified in the previous year. Grim-faced he would then read out that so many people had been changed from coloured to white, so many from white to coloured, so many from Chinese to coloured, from black to coloured, and so on. It was by far the most absurd annual event in Parliament.

One Sunday afternoon I found a Mr Bodenstein and his son-in-law at my front door. Bodenstein had twenty-seven grandchildren; half were classified coloured, the rest white. He thought the time had come to make them all white, and I had to help him. I asked him how on earth he had landed in such a racial cocktail. Just before the Population Registration Act and the Mixed Marriages Act were implemented, he explained, he worked as a steward for the South African Railways. He fell in love with a woman, and before he knew it, she was classified coloured and he white. So he said to himself, to hell with this, and he falsified their marriage certificate. They had a number of children who married all over the colour line, and now he had the mess of his grandchildren. He loved all his grandchildren equally but the coloured ones had to go to inferior schools, live in inferior neighbourhoods and use inferior public amenities, so he felt it would be better if they were all classified white so that there would be no enmity among them. I told him to gather as many of the children and grandchildren together as possible so that I could meet them and talk to them.

One evening after the parliamentary sitting had ended we all found ourselves jammed into the living-room of a house in Woodstock. In my head I was applying article 5.4 (c) to them and I thought to myself that some did not have a hope in hell of becoming white. But when I asked who was white and who coloured, I saw that some of those who looked white were coloured and some who looked coloured were white. Maybe there was a chance after all.

A few days later I caught up with Pen Kotzé, the relevant minister, in the lobby. I told him the story and offered him a proposal. If he made the grandmother white, all the children and grandchildren would automatically become white. If he did not agree, I would see to it that a Bodenstein sob story appeared in the paper every Sunday. Pen is not an unreasonable man and he asked for time to review the case in a sober manner. A week or so later he came back to me and said I had to understand his dilemma; this was, after all, official policy and he could not make so many white all at once. He would make some white now and the rest in six months' time. That was how the Bodensteins became white. They gave me a handsome leather-bound Bible as a gift.

Solomon Brown was a migrant worker from Mozambique, a devout Christian and an elder in his congregation. He and his wife lived for their church. He wanted to become coloured because his wife was; they had been living together for twenty years and I had to help him. I asked him whether there was tension in the congregation concerning him; on the contrary, he said, he and his wife were highly esteemed members. Gently I tried to explain to him that he did not stand a chance in terms of article 5.4 (c), and asked him why he was so determined to be classified coloured. Solomon Brown broke down in tears and with raw emotion explained that the congregation did not know he and his wife were not legally married. He could no longer tolerate this dishonesty before God and the congregation. I told him I was convinced that in the eyes of God he was more of a married man than eighty per cent of the married men I knew, but he remained inconsolable. With little hope and a heavy heart I wrote a motivating letter to the relevant minister. This time it was Connie Mulder, a somewhat scholastic ideologue who was tremendously impressed with his own logic on racial and ethnic identity. Two months later I received an answer. Solomon Brown was a coloured. There was no explanation, except to say that the case had 'merit'.

In my constituency, there was a young coloured artisan who lived with a young white woman. There were always an opened tin of paint and a brush behind the front door. If the neighbours complained and the race-classification inspector came to investigate, he could pretend he had been hired to paint the house.

A young, white Afrikaner man from a prominent family in Oranjezicht pleaded with me to help him become coloured. He had fallen head over heels in love with a Muslim girl; he wanted to become Muslim and coloured immediately so that they could get married. His application failed.

In the new South Africa, Koos van der Merwe is chief whip for the Inkatha Freedom Party. Keppies Niemand is a whip for the NP and Arnold Stofile is chief whip for the ANC, the majority party in the new Parliament. One thing has not changed: in terms of procedure, all parties still jealously guard the time they have available to make speeches. Nobody exceeds the allotted time and it is the task of the whips to see that this does not occur. It is also their duty to beg additional time from other whips when the leader of the party has an important statement to make.

Koos and I were talking over a cup of coffee and he told me that a short while before, Buthelezi had asked him to find an extra ten minutes. Koos said, 'You know, Van Zyl, I first crossed the floor to speak to Keppies Niemand and I asked him if he could spare me a few minutes. You know what he said to me? "F*** off!" Van Zyl, can you believe that a fellow Afrikaner with whom I sat in the same caucus could say such a thing to me?' Koos continued, 'Then I walked across to Arnold Stofile and asked him, "Stoffie, haven't you got a few minutes for me?" You know what he said? "Koos, how much time do you need?" I answered, "Ten minutes." He said, "You've got it." Van Zyl, now that's a white man!' Sometimes I struggle to keep up.

The philosopher Gustav Bergmann claims that an ideological statement is one where a value judgement is presented as a fact. In this sense more ideological statements have probably been made about race or ethnicity than about any other subject. In the name of a specific race or ethnic group, characteristics are claimed and abilities ascribed which bear absolutely no relation to reality.

Oom Bun Booyens, a professor of Afrikaans folk culture many years back, once said, 'You will always recognise an Afrikaner. When the sun sets, he hears the cooing of doves and the rattle of the milk-bucket. He is a rural person to his fingertips.' The fact that more than eighty per cent of Afrikaners had been urbanised at the time he said it did not bother him in the slightest. He wanted Afrikaners to be that way, therefore they were.

These days, *ubuntu* is a property ascribed – almost as a genetic characteristic – to black people. Compassion and love for others are seen as natural characteristics of black people in spite of brutal mass murders in Rwanda, faction fighting in Richmond, KwaZulu-Natal, and senseless taxi murders in various parts of South Africa. Here, there is a clear discrepancy between reality and values. *Ubuntu* is a collective noun for a set of values that are undoubtedly worthy of emulation, but whether these values are indeed embodied by a specific set of people is an empirical question which will be established through investigation and not through *a priori* reasoning.

This reminds me of a discussion with Gerrit Viljoen, then minister of education, and F.W. de Klerk. Gerrit asked me, 'Are you saying that if we get rid of the Population

Registration Act, there will still be Zulus who want to be Zulus?' I replied that it was the only way to find out. Then F.W. asked, 'But what do we do with those Zulus who don't want to be Zulus?' A classic case of what scientific philosopher Alfred North Whitehead would call 'the fallacy of misplaced concreteness'.

This logic was embodied especially in apartheid legislation. Any imposed group identity eventually becomes a contradiction in terms. And now that the Population Registration Act, the Mixed Marriages Act, article 16 of the Immorality Act, the Group Areas Act, and so forth, have been removed, are there still Zulus who want to be Zulus, coloureds who want to be coloureds, whites who want to be whites, Afrikaners who want to be Afrikaners? It is around this question that the principle of freedom of association is unlocking a new dynamic of group identity and cultural self-determination in post-apartheid South Africa.

The fact is that apartheid legislation, despite all pretensions of cultural diversity, used race as a basis for structuring the government system in South Africa. Race as a descriptive characteristic is of questionable value. In biology and anthropology it is useless as an explanatory principle. When used as a classification principle in social relationships, it forms the basis of stereotypes and prejudices. When it is embodied in legislation, it says more about the value judgements of those individuals who make the laws than about those on whom the laws are imposed. To say legally to someone, 'You are coloured, black or white,' says nothing about the person being classified, but rather about what those doing the classification think the person should be. But the 'should' becomes 'is', and so 'race relations' become ideologised. This official obligation then impacts on unofficial relationships and gives them an artificial or forced nature, as in the cases of Bodenstein and Solomon Brown and their wives. Through this process the word 'Afrikaner' became identified with values of exclusive intolerance during the apartheid years. Unlike the case of a coloured, a Bantu or an Indian, there was no law stating who was an Afrikaner. But those who made the apartheid laws were categorically convinced that an Afrikaner had to be white. Considerable consternation arose with the suggestion that coloureds could also be Afrikaners. Apartheid politicised and limited the concept 'Afrikaner'.

And what now? Now that there are no more apartheid laws creating enforced group identities and the principle of freedom of association applies? Who will associate freely with the concept 'Afrikaner'? What social capital in the form of cultural heritage, skills and economic resources can be mobilised to give content to this concept? How will those who linked their Afrikaner identity to the control of political power participate in the process of giving new content to the word 'Afrikaner'? They used and abused political power to consolidate and favour the Afrikaner character (*Afrikanerskap*) as a racial identity. What are most of them going to do now that they have become politically powerless? It will also not help to give new ideological content to Afrikaner identity or to persist with the old associations. If, for example, the ANC and other parties continue to portray Afrikaners as unfeeling white racists, then those thus stereotyped will increasingly feel trapped. This then becomes a self-fulfilling prophecy, as they may well become reactionary in their behaviour towards the new order and undermine it. At the same time, it is unrealistic to portray Afrikaners as a good, well-meaning bunch of people filled with patriotism for the new South Africa.

The term 'Afrikaner' will have to be associated with a

new set of values, but what these are we do not yet know because those who wish to be Afrikaners will have to start moulding and refining these values. And it will not happen overnight either. It cannot take the form of the Sand River Convention at which a set of values is written down and it is then announced that everyone who agrees with them is, as of now, an Afrikaner. And in tailoring new values, people from varied and sometimes unfamiliar backgrounds will participate. People from Rehoboth and Griqualand; Constand Viljoen's people and liberals; the lapsed, the over-enlightened, the rich and the poor. At first we will define each other in and then out as we try to find a sense of community. Whatever the shortcomings of the new dispensation, it has created the space and offered the opportunity for this process to become a reality. How this opportunity is used will determine whether there is a future for Afrikaners in the new South Africa.

One could ask why we should worry at all about the relationship between values and cultural identity. In homogeneous societies one does not encounter the same preoccupation with this question. Danes or Italians seldom, if ever, become self-conscious about which central values are associated with their national identity. But in culturally diverse societies it is a different story, especially if race complicates the issue. The coexistence of minorities within the same political system means that value judgements will inevitably be made. The whole system of apartheid was based on the value-laden point of view that within the same state system there existed irreconcilable interests between minorities and that separate development was, therefore, necessary. Now that apartheid has disintegrated, the debate about values and minorities has again opened up, especially concerning how race and racism can be avoided in value judgements.

According to the literature on the subject, cultural identity is shaped and sustained in two ways: on the one hand, by externally ascribing identity to others and, on the other hand, through internal subjective identification by a person with an imagined or chosen identity. When these processes are consistently at odds with each other, a clash of values develops. Externally ascribed values with which people cannot identify weaken the intensity of group identity. (Jacques Pauw commented that revelations at the Truth and Reconciliation Commission about atrocities committed in the name of Afrikanerdom filled him with such revulsion and aversion that he wanted absolutely nothing to do with the term 'Afrikaner'. This might be his subjective point of view, but it does not mean that he will stop having this term ascribed to him externally. If his aversion were to be reported on in the news, newsreaders would undoubtedly begin with: 'Well-known Afrikaner investigative journalist Jacques Pauw says he does not want to be an Afrikaner.') The challenge for those wishing to be Afrikaners is to bring about a new, common, internal process of value identification that can contribute to a new, external ascription of what being an Afrikaner represents. Society must eventually be able to say, 'To be an Afrikaner means to adhere to or believe in these or those values.' What are these values? That is the question.

It is not just Afrikaners who have to deal with this dilemma. What do the words 'African' and 'African renaissance' mean in the new South Africa? What does the 'new South Africa' mean? All these terms can be given content that reflects values of exclusive intolerance. Can an Afrikaner be an African, or an African an Afrikaner? When we speak of nation-building in South Africa, it is by no means an obvious process. It can either result in a process of exclusive intolerance, where the majority gives an ideological content to being black which excludes from the South African nation those who are not so defined. It could also involve a process whereby society works towards attaining over-arching and transcending values, to which most people in South Africa feel connected, despite their diversity and cultural differences. Which of the two processes becomes predominant will determine South Africa's contribution to the so-called African renaissance or rebirth. But how minorities see themselves will also determine what kind of nation-building takes place in South Africa. If, for example, radical partition is regarded as a precondition for Afrikaner self-determination, then one has to assume from the outset that shared social values are not possible in the new South Africa. Conversely, the philosophical principle that 'a difference has got to make a difference to be a difference' applies, and if it is then said that there exists an identifiable group of people who wish to see themselves as Afrikaners, who are they, and what values do they represent? In the new South Africa it seems to me that, to borrow anthropologist Benedict Anderson's term, they would have to become a new 'imagined community'. Afrikaners will have to apply themselves imaginatively to the task of establishing who they are in the new South Africa. In the process they will have to free themselves from a part of their history and work to create a new one. This is the very challenge that faces South Africa as a nation.

In order to avoid the dilemma associated with the value-laden concept 'Afrikaner', softer, more neutral concepts such as 'Afrikaans-speakers' or 'Afrikaans-users' are used. But however one beats around the bush, the fact is that as a result of our recent past there are Afrikaans-speakers who benefited and Afrikaans-speakers who were harmed, and one was the cause of the other's hardships; one was master and the other servant. The arbitrary dividing line was race, which cut like a knife into the lives of Bodenstein and his family.

There are those who say we have to get away from the concept 'Afrikaner'; who and what it is. It hurts too much, is too divisive and provocative. Let the language be the common denominator. Let us as least cherish and protect that. But the moment you say that the language must be protected, that the promises of the new Constitution must be made applicable to it, it is in essence a political point of view. It has direct implications on education, family life, theatre, the media, business, and so forth. Anthropological literature will show that it is these activities and rituals that characterise communities and with which groups identify or against which they rebel. On this level it is not possible to live as if everything is possible and nothing is essential.

If, for instance, the current government agreed that Afrikaners were those who belong to the independent *volkstaat* Orania, it has direct implications for Afrikaans-speakers who live outside that *volkstaat* and wish to continue doing so. Imagine the government said all Afrikaans-speakers could enjoy full citizenship only in Orania, and the rest were deprived of their civil rights in the new South Africa. Does this not sound familiar? And let us imagine that the Afrikaners of Orania say that Afrikaans-speakers cannot form part of the new South Africa, because their values are irreconcilable with the new order and that their struggle for freedom is being undermined as a result. On whose behalf are they speaking? And if the majority say, 'Not on our behalf, we want to be part of the new order,' how do they want to protect their language and in terms of which values? Or do they say, 'These questions are not important, we simply carry on speaking Afrikaans and hope for the best?'

To say that there are only Afrikaans-speakers or Afrikaans-users and not Afrikaners is actually an ideological pronouncement; in other words, a value judgement presented as a factual statement. This means that there are Afrikaans-speakers who cannot identify themselves with the values of some people who call themselves Afrikaners. In a way this is a negative distancing from certain values, such as racial exclusivity, religious association, and so forth. But what positive identification is there with the values of other Afrikaans-speakers? How and why do they wish to protect and promote the Afrikaans language? And if they can gain clarity on this, how will the rest of society define them? Simply as speakers of Afrikaans? Unlikely.

Why does the term 'Afrikaner' have to be claimed by a small group of people who eliminate by definition other Afrikaans-speakers? Why can the term 'Afrikaner' not include all Afrikaans-speakers who wish to promote Afrikaans as a language by identifying with South Africa as a nation state and with Africa as a continent, without denying their historical roots – whether European, Eastern or African? And then to draw from these cultural origins and to reflect on their role and contribution in the new dispensation, as well as their relationship with other national languages? As a point of departure, this is inclusive tolerance and allows different groups of Afrikaners to take issue with each other about how and why they differ over values, policies and principles. Can there not – as in the case of the Jews or the Scots – be orthodox, progressive, nonbelieving, traditional, modern or even postmodern Afrikaners? Why do Afrikaners steer away from the awkwardness of freeing the term 'Afrikaner' from its undesirable past? Is all this agonising about an exclusive and limited definition even necessary? Why can we not work towards an outcome where the thought of a racist Afrikaner is a contradiction in terms rather than a stereotype? These questions address the history of the term 'Afrikaner' from the Boer War, the establishment of the Union and the 1914 Rebellion right through to apartheid and up to the present. Our society will not afford us the luxury of saying we are Afrikaans-speakers or Afrikaans-users but not Afrikaners. Consistently, the question will be asked: what sort of Afrikaner do you want to be in this new South Africa?

While Afrikaans-speakers and Afrikaans-users are struggling to provide content to their common struggle to let Afrikaans survive, there are a few points we should not lose sight of:

- The new government, in spite of the promises of the Constitution in this regard, has neither the resources nor the infrastructure to provide assistance from government level to help cultural minorities survive. A minority's survival will depend largely on the social and economic capital it can mobilise.
- The new government is exceptionally sensitive and concerned about forging a common South African patriotism; clumsy, vague terms such as 'rainbow nation', 'African renaissance', 'national agenda', and so forth bear testimony to this. Any group that undermines this striving towards transcending values by claiming special minority status can expect considerable conflict and rejection; in other words, even less sympathy for those minority interests.
- There are clear signs of mobilisation along racial lines around concepts such as 'black' and 'African'. Mandela, perhaps unthinkingly, and in spite of the extraordinary, conciliatory role he has played, consistently speaks of 'white', 'coloured', 'Asian' and 'African'. In other words, black = African. Conversely, Mbeki says whites, col-

oureds and Asians are also Africans; this is also the position of the Pan-Africanist Congress. But there are politicians, journalists and academics who bluntly state that African = black and that their millennium has arrived. 'Black' is thus not a descriptive term but rather an ideological and value-laden one. It is ironic that, just as the previous regime said that a South African had to be white, some members of the new order – and this is a growing and influential group – are saying that Africans have to be black. If a minority reacts to this and uses it as a basis for determining its own collective identity, it could lead to racial polarisation and/or ethnic conflict. Here I am thinking especially of politics in the Western Cape and Griqualand. This use of the term 'African' reflects total ignorance of the real state of affairs on the African continent. One has only to think of the people of Algeria, Tunisia, Morocco, the Maghreb, 120 million Muslims, and so forth, to realise how limited and ideologically narrow-minded the obsession with the notion of African as black really is. It appears to be a mixture of Afro-American 'roots nostalgia' and anti-colonial aversion.

- Comparative research clearly shows that minorities in multilingual and multicultural countries who make themselves economically indispensable generally – and I emphasise the word 'generally', bearing in mind the Jews in Germany – survive best and contribute to the general prosperity of the country. This can also become a source of envy and rejection, especially when the minority group forces its economic privileges down the throat of those less privileged. In any event, the general rule that applies here is that the greater a group's knowledge and wealth are, the more transferable and indispensable its skills and prosperity become.

It is almost inevitable that Afrikaans-speakers are going to encounter the consequences of these tendencies when they start reflecting on ways of ensuring the survival of Afrikaans. And when they begin to take up positions concerning survival mechanisms, new values will crystallise which will bring new content to the term 'Afrikaner'. To me this is as plain as a pikestaff. Economic competition, discriminatory citizenship, unequal cultural and social resources, racial or ethnic polarisation – these determine the intensity or lack of conflict in multicultural nations, whether these are the former states of the Soviet Union, Yugoslavia, Rwanda, Nigeria or South Africa. Ultimately, Afrikaans-speakers will be unable to avoid these issues by arranging cosy, comforting gatherings between speakers and users of the language, especially in the context of a new South Africa. Neither the recent past nor the immediate future will offer us this breathing space. What is even more important, though, is that not much is likely to emanate from these meetings that will significantly influence whether Afrikaans survives as a spoken language. Afrikaans-speakers will have to enter their own crucible of truth and reconciliation to determine whether it is feasible to let Afrikaans survive in South Africa.

It is the P.W. Bothas, Andries Treurnichts, Koos van der Merwes, Bodensteins, Solomon Browns, Beyers Naudés, Antjie Krogs, Max du Preezes, Jacques Pauws, Breyten Breytenbachs and so many others who make me ashamed, sad, angry, proud and happy in this country in which I find myself. Who am I? Nothing I have said here or experienced in my life has given me the slightest doubt that, whether I like it or not (and quite separate from my subjective battle), my social identity is also that of an Afrikaner. Consequently, I am as 'Afrikaans' as snoek and sweet potatoes, boerewors and pap. Not a vanguard Afrikaner or a devout, sombre-suited one; not an uptight culture vulture Afrikaner or a free-and-easy, 'alternative', Woodstock one, but a rapidly ageing, confused and sometimes lost Afrikaner, nevertheless. The fact that this has been and remains a source of consternation for some, I have experienced at first hand. But even the consternation is an affirmation of my social identity.

And I developed this identity without conflict or effort. I did not grow up in an 'Afrikaner household'. My parents divorced when my twin sister and I were two years old, and because my mother could not look after us, we were sent to various family members. An English aunt and uncle put us in the Jan Celliers Primary School for grade two and standard one. Hendrik Verwoerd, Nico Diederichs and M.C. Botha (the sons of the well-known fathers) were in my class. There it was made clear to me in no uncertain terms that I did not come from an 'Afrikaner home'. That was in 1948, the year the NP came into power. From there we went to a farm school near Marabastad, twenty-seven kilometres south of Pietersburg. We arrived there when Afrikaner urbanisation and poverty were starting to tail off. These circumstances made it almost a passion to equate being an Afrikaner with being white. Even at that age it did not appeal to me in the slightest. We stayed with my grandparents. My grandfather was a Smuts man and a *Bloedsap*. My father, who had gone off to the war, returned with a hatred for Smuts and joined the NP. My mother had also become a Nat. Because we saw them so seldom, this did not have a significant influence on me. I was a boarder from the age of ten until I got married for the first time. I mention these facts to indicate that there was no systematic influence on my life to make me identify subjectively with being an Afrikaner. Yet it made virtually no difference to my world. From the moment I could think, I was socially identified with being an Afrikaner, even if it was only to say what kind of an Afrikaner I was not.

I have made my peace with the fact that we live in a country where social birthmarks are the order of the day. We are people thrown together in this country, but we are also black, white, coloured, Asian, Indian, Zulu, Xhosa, Tswana, Hindu, Afrikaner, Muslim, English and sometimes a mixture of a number of them. We can only pray for tolerance and open-mindedness as we wrestle with our co-existence in the new South Africa. Without it we will all go mad imagining that this country belongs to one group only. That is a recipe for permanent conflict.

5 Does the Boer Make the Plan or the Plan Make the Boer?

OFTEN WE EXPLAIN THE PRESENT in terms of the future: we find a cause for what is happening now in something that has not yet happened. This is especially true of religious explanations: God's plan or will for the world follows its inevitable course; people are behaving thus now, or history is taking a specific route because God has a plan for the world. That is why there is sense and purpose in what is happening now, even if we do not understand it. But this type of explanation is not confined to religion. Historical determinism, politically and ideologically motivated explanations are logical variations on the same theme. When one speaks of a people's calling, or of the historical responsibility of the working class, or the necessity for a ruling class and that the latter fulfils its duties, there is an element of future inevitability that has a causal impact on what happens now.

The logic of purposeful or teleological explanations is built into most of our explanations of everyday occurrences. The purpose of the heart is to pump blood through the body. Is the purpose the reason for the heart's pumping, or does the pumping result in blood flowing through the body? What are the functions of the liver, pancreas, kidneys, lungs, and so forth? In biological explanations we can use an equilibrium model where a number of interdependent parts contribute to the working of the system as a whole. Once we can define the system in an understandable manner, we can create verifiable conditions under which we can determine whether a specific organ does indeed contribute to the working of the system. Thus we can say, for example, that if body temperature varies outside of a minimum or maximum number of degrees, life will cease, and we can then establish the contributions of the heart, pancreas, kidneys, lungs, and so on, towards stabilising body temperature within these boundaries. Is the purpose of these organs to sustain life, or is life sustained because these organs work the way they do?

There is much debate about verifiable and unverifiable teleological statements. Verifiable teleological statements, in the scientific sense, are statements that can be subjected to test conditions by independent observers. These statements are independently verifiable in the sense that they are not dependent on the religious beliefs, emotions or feelings of a certain person or group of people. There are those who argue that, under such circumstances, there is ultimately no meaningful difference between teleological statements and ordinary causal statements. But how does one test the following statements? 'The future is in God's hands.' 'History is following its predetermined path.' 'The Afrikaner has a calling to fulfil his duty in the south of Africa.' 'The working class has the historical responsibility to lead the unavoidable revolution towards a classless society.' 'The will of Allah will follow its inevitable path in the struggle between believers and non-believers.' In all these declarations a clear future determinism is built in, as if a predetermined plan is the cause of what is happening now. One could argue that it is not the plan that is the cause, but people's faith in the plan. This removes both the explanatory power of the plan and its romanticism. Everyone can believe in what he or she wishes to, and that belief can lead to a wide range of differing actions. But this is not as exciting as to say that your very belief is caused by a plan that will inevitably be realised. The point is simply that if enough people believe wholeheartedly in different plans for the same future, all the ingredients for strife and unhappiness are present. This is the fundamental built-in conflict in monotheistic religions, which see it as their holy duty to claim the world for their god.

But as I have already mentioned, in social discourse, teleological explanations are not confined to religion. One can speak of a secular teleology where a specific outcome in the future is postulated, to which an explanatory power is attributed for today's happenings. Communism, fascism, nationalism and capitalism are secular ideologies that often contain a strong teleological element in their predictions. There is an emotional and even an intellectual appeal in the notion that one is in step with the future and that one's needs are being addressed by an inevitable series of events.

Teleological explanations, whether religious or secular, thus contain a strong eschatological dimension, an expectation of the future. Religion and ideology can, for example, also become intertwined with a national religion: the people are called to do God's will. It does not matter what happens to the people – poverty, adversity, happiness, prosperity – everything can be understood in terms of how God's will is being fulfilled. The problem with religious or secular eschatologies is that they can never be disproved; they remain sufficiently self-explanatory under all circumstances; they are complete tautologies. Neither God nor history can betray itself.

The general appeal of teleological explanations is that they appear to address the problem of meaning and purpose. Between the coincidence of birth and the inevitability of death, people wrestle with the ultimate whys and wherefores of life, and they search for comfort, reassurance and meaning. Nothing is as comforting as the assurance that the uncertainty of the future is managed by the fact that we are in possession of the knowledge to master it. And this unpredictability does not possess the same qualities as scientific uncertainty. It does not matter how much of a grip scientific analysis has on reality and how reliable the knowledge is that has been accumulated, it is still not able to provide any generally acceptable explanation for the reason for my birth and the inevitability of my death. This is where teleological explanations come in and present religious knowledge as fact. It is proper to say that science, ideology and religion should not be mixed, but in people's everyday existence, teleological explanations and eschatological expectations are loaded with the promise of scientific validity. Nobody consults a medium, an astrologer or a fortune-teller without a glimmer of hope that the future might become a little bit more accessible, or is converted without the expectation that God's promises regarding the hereafter will come true. It is this hope and/or expectation that leads to statements like 'it's a miracle', 'that's the way things are', 'everything happens for a reason' or 'don't tempt fate'. It is this attitude which creates the impression that the plan makes the Boer and not the Boer the plan.

Perhaps it is just not possible for people to live meaningfully without unverifiable explanations of reality. An evolutionary explanation of the world, which lacks an aim or a plan, unlocks heated reactions, and when the same logic is transposed to a sort of social Darwinism where it is genetically determined that only the strongest will survive, regardless of people's belief in the future or their moral affiliations, the general sentiment is one of aversion to the meaninglessness of everything. But one should weigh this aversion against the consequences of a fierce, dogmatic belief in the inevitable unfolding of God's plan – especially if your god is not my god and they have different plans for the same world, or your people are not my people and their respective members have an historical responsibility to destroy each other. Was the convenient element of apartheid logic not precisely that the white Afrikaner people at the southern tip of Africa were called to lead other peoples towards separate maturity? And is this not the same logic as that upon which the historical responsibility of the working class to lead the world towards a classless existence is based?

The examples offered so far do not appear terribly sophisticated, but the influence of teleological arguments in extremely abstract and theoretical explanations of social reality is fairly widespread. Usually one variation on systems theory or another is used to create an analytical framework within which economic behaviour or problems of social order are explained. A system is postulated to which certain systemic objectives are ascribed and social processes are then explained in terms of the function or purpose they fulfil for the system as a whole. The analogy of an organism, borrowed from biology, is even used to explain how certain social organs contribute to the functioning of institutions like the state, the community or the market. In this way one can then look at the functions of crime, social deviation, price fluctuations or similar social processes for society as a greater organism. Such a seemingly passionless, objective analysis of society, clad in biological rhetoric, lends a quasi-scientific validity to the analysis. The difference is, however, that in biology clear test conditions can be set, allowing one to predict and explain when an organic system will die or when one of its organs will no longer function. In social analysis the argument too often drifts into a tautology of the kind where a system stops functioning when its parts are no longer contributing to its integration, or a part of society will stop functioning when it no longer contributes to the whole.

But if we dispense with unverifiable teleology, does this inevitably lead to a meaningless world? The fact that I do not have the final answer definitely does not mean that there is no answer. And if I cannot base a moral code on absolutely predictable and secure beliefs, does this mean that I must live amorally or immorally? Why can one not take responsibility for one's own moral position? Is it not preferable to accept yourself freely as the final source of your convictions and judgements without placing the guilt or responsibility on God, history, your ethnic origin, social standing or the class system? There are too many examples in history of atrocities for which people have laid the blame and responsibility on powers beyond their control. This is a world in which individual fallibility and error disappear and accountability becomes relative to circumstances, context and social ties. Everyone sounds off about what responsibility means but nobody wants to be accountable.

I am deeply sceptical of teleological explanations, whether of a moral or so-called scientific nature. That is why I am suspicious of any ideology, religion or analytical scheme that removes the need for people to take responsibility for their own judgements and behaviour. The kind of society in which I wish to live, and for which I am prepared to work, even to make sacrifices, is one in which no preternatural intellectual crutches are required to make sense of my existence, the workings of society or the course of history. The abiding virtue in the search for knowledge and meaning is doubt, an incessant return to questioning and explanation. My values and ethical judgements must be tested continually against my experiences and my actions. I must recognise and admit my shortcomings in terms of my own values and ethics. Remorse and apology are not prerequisites for forgiveness. Forgiveness is the prerogative of the victim and stands apart from my own accountability. I apologise because I harmed myself, because I abused my own judgement and sense. Or because my morality was faulty or I acted contrary to it. But this is virtually impossible to acknowledge if I start off by deciding that my judgements and actions are based on values and standards determined outside the human plane, or that they result from a social system of which I am merely an unknowing extension.

I know that the phenomenon of cultural diversity makes such tenets problematic. Concepts such as honour, courage and honesty – on an ethical level – and truth, valid knowledge and reliable prediction – on an explanatory level – are loaded with culturally relative meanings. This is probably one of the causes of postmodernist pessimism and nihilism. But cultural relativism cannot be equated with intellectual relativism, in spite of the fact that a specific intellectual tradition – science, for example – has taken stronger root in some cultural contexts than in others. It is an illusion to search for an analytical point of departure that is totally independent of culture and from which I can confirm the truth and moral validity of all culturally relative positions, including my own. It would be the height of cultural arrogance. That is why, quite simply, to me it is a given that, from within a constantly renewing cultural standpoint, I profess that I am responsible for my own judgements and actions and that no one else carries the blame. This is how it is for me and this is the basis on which I wish to be judged.

6 The Struggle

IT WAS SOME TIME BEFORE I realised that the fight against apartheid was not synonymous with the struggle. One could do things to strengthen or help the struggle, even believe in some of its goals, without being accepted. The fight against apartheid within the struggle solidified between fixed ideological boundaries wherein strategic and tactical dogmatism demanded total and uncritical loyalty from its members. It had its own heroes, shaped its own myths, and wrote and rewrote its own history. The changes the struggle prescribed for South Africa had an inherent teleological inevitability, which did not tolerate any scepticism or doubt, and one's ethical standing was determined by the struggle's judgement of how reconcilable one's actions were with its own aims. The struggle's fight against apartheid sanctified, forgave and justified everything. In its terms one could lie, steal, torture, commit murder or perjury, and encourage corruption, because once apartheid was beaten, the necessity for all these things would vanish and combatants of the struggle would live in circumstances under which this lack of personal accountability would no longer be necessary. This lack of moral accountability applied in even greater measure to those who tried to destroy the struggle, namely the apartheid establishment. The apartheid establishment's fight against the struggle sanctified, forgave and justified everything. In its terms you could lie, steal, torture, commit murder or perjury, and encourage corruption, as long as the battle could be waged. Connie Mulder once said that when it came to survival, 'the game has no rules'. But the difference was that apartheid was 'evil' and the struggle was 'holy'; therefore the sins of the struggle could be justified and forgiven. Apartheid was a 'crime against humanity', one of those convenient moral shibboleths that assume common understanding.

What I do know is that when the two sides started negotiating with each other – something both had opposed to the death and swore would never happen – we sat down with some sanctified crooks, murderers and liars who had to make the new South Africa work, irrespective of how holy or unholy their fight against each other had been. Suddenly they had to commit themselves, and all of us, to transparency, accountability, justice, human rights, equal rights for women, the eradication of corruption, the abolishment of the death penalty, truth and reconciliation and any other virtue imaginable. But their entire fight against each other had been based on precisely the opposite of all these virtues. Perhaps it would have been better if the struggle had won an absolute victory, because then we might have been able to start from scratch. But a negotiated transition only underlined the fact that this was not possible. How does one reconcile lies with truth, murder with no death penalty, corruption with accountability, justice with injustice; and this by means of an outmoded state structure – now shared between two antagonists in order to give content to the new South Africa – which was systematically and purposefully honed to undermine this desired new morality? It should come as no surprise that our criminal justice system is in crisis and that crime is flourishing.

But before one becomes too cynical, it would be a good idea to remember that the struggle was born to eradicate racism and oppression in South Africa and to replace it with a nonracial, nondiscriminatory society. And there were not only thugs and crooks; there were a great many people who tackled apartheid with enormous sacrifice and courage, and who never foisted their struggle credentials upon you. Zanele Mbeki is one of these: feet firmly on the ground, without vanity or airs and graces. In this sense the struggle was an inherent and important part of the greater fight against apartheid, even if there were those who were convinced that the struggle was the only truly legitimate fight. Consequently, it was almost inevitable that anyone who opposed apartheid at some stage or another would either come into contact with the struggle or be judged by it.

I still look back with a great deal of astonishment at my almost limitless naïveté regarding the organisation, ideology and actions of the struggle when I entered Parliament in 1974. By then I had a well-developed intellectual and moral aversion towards the ideology and practice of apartheid. While I never for a second thought that white, parliamentary politics was the only suitable platform from which to dismantle apartheid, I believed that it could nevertheless be a useful means to make individual protest and to expose the atrocities of the system. Of course students at the various English-medium universities where I had lectured up to then had strong views about the irrelevance of parliamentary politics, but for me student politics was neither more nor less irrelevant than parliamentary politics, and the latter had greater continuity and was less vulnerable than the former.

Only in retrospect did I realise that in 1974 the struggle was rather disorganised and far less hegemonic than it would later become. At that stage, black consciousness, as depicted in the works and writings of Steve Biko in

South Africa and Frantz Fanon and Stokely Carmichael elsewhere, was the order of the day and that, by definition, excluded me from participation. I still remember the trauma and pain with which the National Union of South African Students (NUSAS) experienced the breakaway of black students from its ranks and the joy this gave some Nationalists. Even the Soweto uprising of 1976 caught the ANC and the struggle by surprise. Some exiles later told me that it felt to them as if they had become irrelevant to the internal struggle against apartheid.

Nothing gave the struggle greater impetus than the South African government's two-pronged process of internal cruel oppression and external military aggression. Within the country the struggle began to consolidate resistance outside conventional parliamentary politics; abroad it began to isolate the South African government dramatically. This isolation coincided with the heating up of the Cold War in the late 1970s and early 1980s, and exacerbated the growing ideological polarisation between the East (communism) and the West (capitalism). The South African Communist Party was a surrogate of the Soviet Union's Communist Party and was also strategically placed within the ANC and the struggle. Out of this the comrade culture, with its clear ideological and strategic preferences, was born. Between the mid-1970s and mid-1980s, a clear revolutionary strategy began to crystallise within the struggle. This later became known as the National Democratic Revolution (NDR), with four critical sub-elements: armed struggle, international isolation (sanctions), underground internal action and internal mass mobilisation. It was during this time that I began my parliamentary career and, as a result of my participation in Parliament, I was regarded as a potential political enemy of the struggle. The United Democratic Front (UDF), later the Mass Democratic Movement (MDM), was eventually the total manifestation of the struggle's internal strategy of underground action and mass mobilisation. The MDM internally and the ANC externally determined the legitimate struggle, strategies and tactics against apartheid and they constantly discussed these among themselves.

As the Total Strategy of the National Party and the NDR of the struggle began to polarise in relation to each other, ordinary people who were not part of either found themselves caught in the cross-fire. The smallest everyday action was seen by one of the two sides as either undermining the system or undermining the struggle. To buy cooking oil during a trade boycott could lead to a necklace murder; if a student were to say that he or she wanted to communicate with the ANC abroad, it could lead to the confiscation of a passport. A climate of intense mistrust and collusion ensued. Any individual initiative outside the NDR strategy for the struggle was viewed with displeasure, even hostility. Like, for example, my attempt at starting up a national convention movement internally. The idea was to bring together all parties and organisations that were in favour of negotiations between the ANC and other parties, but particularly the NP government, to form a pressure group that aimed to bring about negotiations. People like Allan Boesak and even Desmond Tutu were initially in favour but when the word came from Lusaka that such a movement would weaken revolutionary fervour and could even be a sly strategy of the Botha regime, the MDM pulled out. That was the death knell for the initiative.

Nothing in this context caused greater inner turmoil than compulsory military service or conscription. The struggle, for understandable reasons, targeted it as the test for white commitment to the fight against apartheid. Initially I tried to defend national service by arguing that this was the shield behind which transformation and negotiation would have to take place, and that these processes were impossible in the prevailing context of anarchic violence. But the more the National Security Management System (NSMS) unfolded, the weaker and less convincing my argument became. The NSMS was the operational plan of the Botha government's Total Strategy. Internally it was applied ruthlessly to oppress 'enemies of the state' and even to eradicate them, and beyond South Africa's borders it hunted down the ANC in exile and destabilised neighbouring states. Ultimately it was the NSMS that made my continued participation in parliamentary politics untenable.

But my resignation did not mean that I was now an unquestioning supporter of the NDR and the armed struggle. This was something a whole bunch of comrades just could not figure out. In their view, you were either with them or against them because, as Joe Slovo used to say, 'there is no middle ground' (the title of one of his many articles on revolutionary strategy). National service was used by the struggle as justification for their range of armed resistance; farmers on farms, clients in nightclubs or cafés were targets equally as valid as soldiers or the police. The dividing line between civilians and the military vanished and terror was a valid tactic to overthrow the *status quo*. In the same way it became an equally valid tactic for the establishment to defend the *status quo*. The country polarised into two camps of competing ruthlessness. All of this was revealed in evidence brought before the Truth and Reconciliation Commission (TRC).

It was in this climate, after the failed attempt to bring to life the national convention movement, that I decided in 1985 to take the executive committee of my party to Lusaka to meet the top leaders of the ANC. It was, after all, they who had destroyed the initiative and we wanted to find out for ourselves what they had in mind. This was my first encounter with the architects of the struggle. To say that I was overwhelmed would be putting it mildly. Mac Maharaj, Thabo Mbeki, Alfred Nzo, Gertrude Shope … A whole new area of history opened up for me, an awareness of my insulation in the fight against apartheid, a feeling of intense camaraderie and common objectives. With hindsight one realises how infinitely more accomplished they were as politicians; to what extent it was part of their daily existence to charm a wide variety of people from all over the world and to make them a part of the struggle. In a certain sense we were novices and like putty in their hands.

During the first meeting the sole focus was on the objectives of the struggle, its overwhelming moral validity, and their and many others' hardship in its service. There was virtually no discussion on strategy or tactics, except that one was repeatedly made aware of the doubtful value of anything tried from 'within the system', and especially within parliamentary politics. My plea that peaceful transition would ultimately be impossible without significant white participation was received with polite but dismissive smiles. At that stage the ANC had long since stopped considering peaceful transition an option. In retrospect I see that this was the first point at which I realised I was not really perceived as being part of the struggle, and that if they could not make me a part of it on their terms, I should at least be neutralised as far as any competing options of opposition to apartheid over which the struggle had no control were concerned. But a lot of water still had to flow under the bridge before this insight crystallised.

The 1987 Dakar gathering was an emotionally exhausting

experience. This time it was not a party-political delegation. Breyten Breytenbach, Alex Boraine and I recruited delegates widely and on an extremely personal level, mainly among Afrikaans-speaking people in journalistic, academic, business and art circles. In Dakar we spent ten days almost exclusively debating tactics and strategy. Yes, was the position of the ANC, we accept that you genuinely oppose apartheid, but what are you going to do about it? This caused great turmoil and division among the group from South Africa. The central issue was that of the armed struggle and sanctions against the South African government. It was not enough to say that one understood how it happened that people were driven to take up arms; the ANC wanted unqualified support for its strategies and tactics. This it could not obtain and so the focus shifted and we concentrated on our particular commitment and devotion to the fight against apartheid. What does it mean in your personal capacity when you say that you are going to protest against apartheid? Participation in Parliament, military service, public protests, mobilisation of support for the ANC? And through it all one felt defenceless and vulnerable, as if one's own contribution was so insignificant compared with the sacrifices the political exiles were making. Mac Maharaj hobbled around with a cane. When asked about it, he said it was the result of continuous torture at the hands of the South African security police. Later, during CODESA negotiations, he laughingly told me it was all a ruse to mislead us by pretending that he was on his way to Moscow to receive medical treatment, whereas he was in fact on his way to South Africa to launch Operation Vula, an underground resistance operation.

After ten days we were exhausted. We devised a flimsy statement wherein we committed ourselves to doing everything in our power to fight apartheid. I do not think any of us doubted that this was not good enough to qualify as being part of the struggle as the ANC saw it. The fact that the meeting itself played an important role in ending the politics of force and legitimising negotiations with the ANC only dawned on both us and them much later. But, again, much water first had to flow under the bridge.

While we were in Dakar, the ANC blew up the Witwatersrand Command Headquarters and caused considerable damage. P.W. Botha and Magnus Malan were furious and said this was the ANC's way of thanking me for our grovelling safari to the ANC. (Oliver Tambo apologised to me a few months later in Lusaka for the embarrassment and assured me that it had not been done deliberately.) It was a difficult time and clear lines were drawn in the sand to distinguish between various people's strategic alliance in the fight against apartheid. Hein Grosskopf, a good Afrikaner from an establishment Afrikaner family, was held responsible for the explosion and Adriaan Vlok, minister of police, issued a reward for his arrest. I protested against both the explosion and the accusation without evidence against Grosskopf, a position of no consequence in the battle between the struggle and the system. In the meantime, Boraine and I continued to organise meetings with the ANC outside South Africa's borders: in Lusaka, Harare, Victoria Falls, Leverkusen, Frankfurt, Bonn, London, New York and Paris. It did not necessarily qualify us as part of the struggle, but in the end every little bit helped.

To me these meetings and conferences had two main achievements: a relatively intimate insight into the lives of some of the struggle's top foot soldiers and an appreciation of the differences and rivalry between the various elements and factions involved. There was, without doubt, an extraordinary camaraderie and goodwill between them, which infected me. In spite of the seriousness of the times we devoted considerable time to pleasure and relaxation. There was drinking and partying, often to the early hours. In vino veritas discussions took place frequently and passionately and we all allowed ourselves to be vulnerable. As a result, I was relatively well fortified emotionally against the mythologising of personalities after negotiations for the new South Africa had been concluded and the new crowd had to start governing. One has only to think back to one or two incidents in Paris or Lusaka or wherever to secularise the new myths immediately. Perhaps it is easier to be charismatic and morally unblemished after 27 years of imprisonment than to move from one hotel and conference to the other with sex, adulation and alcohol readily available. As sociologist Peter Berger pointed out years ago, it is difficult to maintain dignity with your pants around your knees.

Gradually I became aware that there were different dividing lines and power crises within the struggle. The official position was that all hearts beat as one, and that the solidarity and discipline were collective and indivisible, but it did not take long to realise that there were competitive ranks and turfs. One can still speak broadly of the imprisoned, internal and exiled leadership (initially Nelson Mandela in prison, Cyril Ramaphosa internally and Oliver Tambo in exile, but with the retirement of Mandela, Ramaphosa's departure from politics and the demise of Tambo, Mbeki is currently lord of the manor). I say broadly, because within these divisions there were subdivisions. Though these divisions created their own cliques and loyalties, their potential ferocity was transcended by the all-embracing goal of eradicating apartheid. But when that eventually happened, it was a totally different story. The struggle moved from the fight against apartheid to one for control of the ANC. In the process, a new ruling establishment is being shaped, fascinating to observe.

With the emergence of this new establishment the boundaries of the struggle are being redefined according to the wishes of the upcoming leadership. Some are 'in', others 'out' – regardless of how great or important their fight against apartheid had been. Take the case of Beyers Naudé: he was under house arrest, was rejected by his church, worked day and night to help hundreds of the persecuted and oppressed, and literally raised millions of rands to help pay for the struggle both internally and externally. He was part of the Groote Schuur delegation of the ANC, but when, shortly thereafter, he said he was not a card-carrying member of the ANC, he vanished without trace in the negotiations that followed. In the meantime business people who, even if they were not in favour of apartheid, at least did almost nothing to fight it, nearly broke their golf clubs to ingratiate themselves with the inner circle of the new leadership. Many tried but few succeeded, even if they did donate money to the Mandela Children's Fund, attended smart fundraising dinners on Robben Island or rebuilt special schools at which the struggle leaders had been educated as children. Bill Venter even funded the Bram Fischer library and officially opened it. Imagine that: an honorary colonel of the thirty-second battalion! Bey Naudé could have told them it is not that easy. The leadership decides in its own way who is to be blessed and who rejected, and every new leadership decides in its own way. That is why the definitive history of the struggle will never be written; new heroes will be discovered and old myths will vanish.

There was a time before the start of negotiations and during them when I naïvely, even romantically, believed that the ANC under Mandela and Mbeki would mobilise talent inclusively and broadly to turn the ship of the new South Africa around, because it would take all the talents and skills available to us to get it right quickly. But I had forgotten my Machiavelli and Pareto. Ultimately, just as with the old regime, it is all about the power of patronage and favouritism; about clientelism and protectionism; about the circulation of the élite and new public servants and sycophants, the whole utterly boring lot of them. Privilege, status, power and pomp become the barometers of change and transformation, and the same tired, hackneyed, racist, pseudo-patriotic arguments are used to establish the boundaries of loyalty and inner-circle favouritism. But I know that Thabo is too shrewd not to spot this problem. The *oubaas* had perhaps been isolated for too long to notice them. In any case, every now and then it seems he has tamely submitted to them.

My own fitting in within the new dispensation was, and still is, uncomfortable. I am still not a member of any political party since walking out of the old Parliament. My experiences as a member of the Progressive Federal Party taught me that membership is not a step to take lightly. Your independence becomes undermined by party and caucus discipline and you often have to defend the indefensible. I was, for example, opposed from the outset to the qualified franchise of the Progressive Party, which was based on the principle that only people who had attained a certain level of formal education – for example, standard eight – should have the vote. I was awkward and unhappy in justifying this and I immediately began working to remove it from party policy. The experience of being a party member convinced me never again to compromise my intellectual independence for membership of any organisation.

Since 1989 a few transitional processes have occupied

my time. I was chairman of the Metropolitan Chamber, a mediating body founded by Cyril Ramaphosa and Olaus van Zyl of the NP to end the rent boycott in Soweto in exchange for the establishment of a nonracial local government structure; this took up three years of my life. From 1995 to 1996 I was co-chairman with Khehle Shubane of the task group charged with organising local government elections. But both the ANC and De Klerk made it clear to me, unasked, that they did not see a role for me in the negotiation process. For one reason or another there was the assumption that I wanted to appropriate such a role for myself.

My most bizarre experience of this situation was my brief involvement with the South African Broadcasting Corporation (SABC). I was on my way back from Swaziland when I heard on the radio that F.W. de Klerk had, without consulting me, appointed me chairman of the SABC board. I immediately called my secretary from the car and asked her to issue a press statement saying that I was embarrassed by the way the appointment was made and that I did not accept it.

I had scarcely arrived home, towards six that afternoon, when the phone calls started. First it was Pallo Jordan saying that I should not accept the appointment; then Mandela saying that accepting it could seriously damage my reputation and that I was doing excellent work at the Metropolitan Chamber; then De Klerk who was upset that I did not want to accept the position. De Klerk asked me to meet him the next day in Cape Town. In his office he made an urgent appeal to me to at least call the board's first meeting so that it be constituted. I agreed. Mandela phoned repeatedly, asking me to resign immediately, and warning me that if I did not, I would be seen as 'De Klerk's man'. I explained that I would call the first meeting only, at which I would resign. Mandela sounded mistrustful and unhappy.

At the meeting on the twenty-ninth floor of the SABC building, I announced my resignation. There was unanimous opposition. By resigning, the board members said, I was putting them all in an awkward position, because technically they were all De Klerk's appointees. Moreover, they needed time to decide on my successor. It would be selfish of me to walk away, and they asked that I stay on for at least three weeks. At the press conference following the meeting, I announced that I would stay on just long enough for my successor to be chosen. Then the fat was really in the fire. Mandela continued to contact me and exerted pressure on me to resign. The ANC and De Klerk got into an ugly public fight about it all.

I had to go to Dakar and while I was there, I heard about secret meetings by ANC members – Fatima Meer (a board member), Allister Sparks, Ray Louw and others – plotting to get rid of me. It was becoming totally ridiculous. From Dakar I convened an emergency meeting to be held as soon as I arrived back in South Africa. During the meeting I pointed out that I had stayed on as chairman at the unanimous request of the board, that I had wished to resign at the first meeting, and that it was totally unnecessary for secret meetings to be held at which it was plotted to get rid of me. Fatima, whom I have known for many years, said I should understand it made no difference what my personal contribution to democratisation in South Africa had been, 'the people would not tolerate a white Afrikaner male in that position'. I immediately announced my resignation and shortly thereafter my participation as board member as well. Mandela phoned to thank me personally and to convey his appreciation for my generosity of spirit. Ivy Matsepe-Casaburri became chairperson in my place. She was appointed in precisely the same manner as I had been by De Klerk, without consultation or agreement. She, however, had the correct political birthmarks: a woman, black, and part of the struggle.

To a lesser or greater extent, I had similar experiences while I was chairman of the Metropolitan Chamber and co-chairman of the task group responsible for arranging local government elections. As soon as I adopted a position the struggle clique found unacceptable, I was 'white', 'racist' or 'part of the system'. The struggle won the battle for power and control. But the battle against racism, intolerance, nepotism, wasted resources, small-mindedness and corruption continues.

I do not believe that Mbeki and the leadership of the ANC are 'soft' on these issues. It would be just too superficial and artificial to play such politics. But it is not that easy to get rid of established interests in the struggle or to resist the temptation of patronage and favouritism when influence and power are being competed for. These are often the foundations used to build a new establishment.

In the first five years, Mandela could ignore these problems to a large extent because he focused on symbolic reconciliation politics, which was closely linked to his personality. While he was doing this, a bitter struggle for control of the ANC was going on. Mbeki won the battle by means of patronage, favouritism, cunning and manipulation. That is how it is in politics. His struggle came home, was weaned from liberation and now he has to govern. Often, in such cases, what were formerly advantages and ammunition become a noose around the neck.

7 The New in the Old and the Old in the New

ONE SHOULD REMEMBER THAT the term 'liberal democracy' is a normative concept. Those who believe in it are bound to a certain set of principles of which constitutional government, the sovereignty of law, protection of individual rights through a constitutional court, adult franchise and the separation of administrative, judicial and executive powers are among the most important. When a liberal democracy becomes entrenched within the constitution of a country, as in the case of South Africa, it creates a normative framework within which government must take place. But it also obliges citizens under the authority of the constitution to honour these values in their behaviour, even if they do not really believe in them. At the same time, a liberal democratic constitution assumes, or implies, quite a few supporting structures to give practical expression to its goals, such as an effective criminal justice system (courts, police, jails) and a fairly effective civil service to provide basic services such as education, health, housing, and so forth. Some say a free market system and independent civil society are also necessary.

This concept of democracy is currently the dominant one in international politics. When mention is made of a process of democratisation, it is accepted that a country is on its way to a mature liberal democratic dispensation. Several countries in Latin America, Southeast Asia, Africa, Eastern Europe and the states of the former Soviet Union are caught up in this process. So is South Africa. It might seem obvious, but not so long ago the word 'democracy' was used to refer to 'democratic centralism', as in the Soviet Union and in Eastern Europe; 'one-party democracy', as in some African countries (Yoweri Museveni of Uganda speaks of a 'no-party democracy' for his country); and 'populist democracy' (with variations of participatory, assembly or direct democracy), as was the case with some Latin American countries. All these variations reflected a different value system from that assumed in a liberal democracy. In fact, there are social democrats who say that a liberal democracy is in conflict with, or even the opposite of, democratic principles.

I make these distinctions to underline the fact that the choice of a particular form of democracy means a choice for the selective emphasis of certain values. Today a liberal democracy is the dominant paradigm for what a democracy should be, as a result of factors such as the fall of organised communism in 1989, the ensuing leading international role of established democracies in the United States, the United Kingdom, Western Europe, Scandinavia, Canada, New Zealand and Australia, as well as the role of Bretton Woods institutions like the World Bank and the International Monetary Fund (IMF). In this era, to speak of a country as being undemocratic is to express a value judgement from within this perspective. To say today that a country is striving towards being democratic is an invitation to analyse it according to the normative assumptions of a liberal democracy.

The normative dimension of democracy makes it almost inevitable that it will become caught up in ideological debates. For example, a liberal democracy emphasises the primary importance of the individual and the protection of the individual's rights. How can this value judgement be reconciled with that of the self-determination of minorities and group rights like language, culture and religion? It is all very well to argue that by protecting the rights of the individual, group rights are protected, but what happens when a specific group's values undermine the rights of the individual outside that group? How does a democratically elected government handle the conflict that arises?

Another case is that affirmative action cannot take place without discriminating on the basis of race, even though the Constitution specifically says that one may not discriminate on these grounds. This conflict is justified in several ways, notably by saying that the victims of previous discrimination must now enjoy positive discrimination. No matter how it is done, the result is that race and racial issues will remain an inherent part of a liberal democratic dispensation in South Africa through deliberate policy implementations.

A further example of ideological or value conflict is the position that capitalism can flourish without a democracy – but a democracy cannot be sustained without a capitalist economy. If a competitive market economy is an inherent part of government policy, as is the case in South Africa, it must inevitably create tension with organised unions that use socialism as their basic point of departure. In South Africa, the greatest ideological tension is experienced over the formulation of economic policy *within* the ANC alliance, where the official policy of the government is that of a strong, competitive market economy, while the South African Communist Party (SACP) and the Congress of South African Trade Unions (COSATU) are firmly committed to a state-led socialist economy. The political space a liberal democracy creates makes it possible for interest groups to further positions that undermine the principles of a liberal democracy. These are normally justified in terms of values other than those associated with a liberal democracy.

The tension between reality and values is evident in the mutual relationships of goals that the government has set for the country. These goals are justified in terms of values usually associated with a liberal democracy. So there is, for example, a simultaneous pursuit of the consolidation of a democracy and that of a sustainable market economy. The former creates expectations of equal rights; the latter results in inequality of material outcomes. The economic transformation needed to promote a market economy causes short-term deprivation for a large part of the population, who have the opportunity afforded them in the new political arena to manifest their discontent. The removal of exchange controls, privatisation, reducing the country's debt burden, and the development of a more flexible labour market are all measures that create tensions between the ANC and its associates. At the same time, the government really has no other choice than to do this, if it wants South Africa to fit into the current international economy. In the case of South Africa there is an inherent tension between the imperative of a growing market economy and the expectations created by a liberal democracy.

The government wants to establish a human rights culture and, at the same time, it wants to maintain strict law and order. These two values do not necessarily exclude each other logically, but the practical relationship between them is not self-evident. The police, courts, correctional services and government are constantly faced with difficult choices. How does one reconcile the rights of victims, or the community, with those of criminals? If this tension between laws and law and order has a weakening effect on the workings of the criminal justice system, the public loses faith in the government's capacity to ensure safety, and this strengthens the tendency to take the law into one's own hands through vigilantism or to privatise security services.

The government wants both to exercise fiscal discipline and to deliver services to the population. In light of the current debt burden of the state as well as the fact that the civil service payroll conveniently made up more than one third of the 1999 budget, this means that discretionary space for state spending is extremely limited. From the IMF, the World Bank and foreign investors there is the expectation that the government will keep the deficit at three per cent. In short, even if the departments of education, housing, health, and so forth were the most efficient in the world – and they are not – there is far too little money available for them to meet even a small part of the promises made to the population. Still, government can hardly say that it will not deliver services, and at the same time it is obliged to exercise fiscal discipline.

Democracy, economic growth, human rights, law and order, fiscal discipline and service delivery are all 'good' values. To choose or prioritise among them is not to choose between good and bad. It is ridiculously easy to choose between good and bad; it is extremely difficult to choose between good and good. The concurrent striving for all these by government, and the need constantly to prioritise in favour of one at the expense of another, creates a climate of uncertainty and confusion. It is not necessarily a matter of government not knowing what it wants; it is rather a matter of government wanting to achieve too much at once. Within the current South African context, attempts to consolidate democracy can be a source of instability.

Stability is the magic word for investors, Western governments and the World Bank. It means predictability, sustainability, the reasonable assumption that faith in the medium- to long-term future has not been misplaced. Stability is one of the cardinal ingredients for faith in the economy and government of a country. If you correlate democracy with stability, you get four ideal typical or hypothetical possibilities: democratic stability, undemocratic stability, democratic instability and undemocratic instability. Each can be used to analyse actual situations. Thus it is generally accepted that America, Britain, Germany, Scandinavia, Australia, Canada and New Zealand are examples of democratic stability; at different stages Latin American countries like Brazil, Argentina, Chile and Mexico were regarded as examples of democratic instability, and the Belgian Congo, Sudan and Somalia as examples of undemocratic instability. Countries where undemocratic stability prevailed are usually divided into market-friendly countries (Taiwan, South Korea, Chile under Pinochet, Singapore) and market-unfriendly countries (Cuba, the former Eastern European communist countries, the states of the Soviet Union, China under Mao). Each of these countries can be analysed to establish what the structural circumstances were which either furthered or undermined stability and/or democracy. Out of these then flow prescriptions for what a country should do to become more stable and/or more democratic.

Capitalists and investors are primarily concerned with stability. One of the most common misrepresentations of the twentieth century was that they cared about democracy and the values associated with it. The historical evidence is overwhelming that they could not care less. Their primary goal is to make money, not to make democracy work. They invested in Nazi Germany, Fascist Italy, Communist China, one-party military dictatorships, and so forth, for as long as they were convinced that there was sufficient stability to protect the profit on their investments. Consequently, when a financial analyst gives pious advice to a South African minister of finance about how economic growth can be fostered and confidence shaped in the country, it has absolutely nothing to do with how a democracy will be consolidated in South Africa. The most common advice to which the South African government has to listen virtually every day is, for example: abolish exchange controls immediately, get rid of the grip of organised labour, privatise at once, and reduce the deficit as much as possible. The resultant capital flight, political labour unrest, unemployment as a result of privatisation and the lack of funds to improve services, as well as the demands they make on a young democratising country, do not bother them in the slightest. If it requires a high degree of market-friendly undemocratic stability to achieve this, it just has to be done. The choice is between investment and economic growth, and no investments and no growth. This dilemma is one of the strongest influences on the economic policy of the South African government, which flows from the globalising international economy.

It is worth noting that the encouragement to simultaneously democratise and stimulate market-driven economic growth comes mostly from countries where democratic stability prevails and where there is no inherent tension between the two objectives. Consequently, when the World Bank and the IMF speak of 'combining good governance with sound management of the economy', the explicit or implicit model they have in mind is that of the mature democracies of the United States and Western Europe. The dilemma, of course, is that the supporting institutions and socio-economic infrastructure in these countries, which strengthen the relationship between a market economy and a democratic political system, are largely absent, or, as in the case of South Africa, are still in an underdeveloped state.

The sources of instability lie not only in the simultaneous pursuit of 'good' goals that could undermine each other. They can also be found in factors like the enormous gap between the wealthy minority and the majority of poor people; the accelerated pace of uncontrolled urbanisation; and the lack of sufficient housing, good education and health services. Two internal factors that need to be singled out in this context are the phenomenon of a 'weak state' and the conflict between the modern and the traditional. The concept 'weak state' refers to the fact that when a society moves relatively peacefully by means of negotiation from an undemocratic to a democratic dispensation, state institutions become weaker before, or if, they become stronger. This is because they have to be transformed and deliver services simultaneously. In practical terms, the old civil servants of the former regime, as well as the civil service culture upheld by them, must now become subservient to the culture of a liberal democracy and help train the new officials.

Nowhere is this more strikingly obvious than within South Africa's criminal justice system. The maintenance of law and order revolves around three basic activities: how a criminal is arrested, how a criminal is prosecuted in court, and how a criminal serves his or her sentence. The departments responsible for these functions in South Africa are themselves undergoing a process of fundamental transformation and are, furthermore, not well synchronised. As a result, the lack of law and order in South Africa is becoming an important source of instability and is identified as a problem without exception by potential investors. The state is, by virtue of its functions – upholding the law, providing education and health services, and so on – the only and most important service-delivery instrument of a government. When this instrument is weak or unreliable, it undermines the workings of a democratic constitution. Ultimately, if it cannot become an effective instrument of service delivery, the state becomes increasingly criminalised and a source of corruption and crime. In extreme cases, the state becomes a kleptocracy, which is used by a ruling élite to plunder society, as was the case in Zaïre under Mobutu.

Inasmuch as there was political violence after 1990, it was found in Zulu-on-Zulu and, to a lesser degree, in Xhosa-on-Xhosa conflicts. There was very little, if any, inter-ethnic or inter-racial violence. The most important threat, of rightwing Afrikaner conflict, never materialised. Every case of political violence requires its own specific investigation, but a common theme in intra-ethnic violence relates to the tension between modernity and traditionalism. Inherited traditional leadership stands in direct opposition to liberal-democratic elected leadership. Leadership is symptomatic of deep-seated differences about values that have to do with family relationships, marriage, the status of women, land ownership, settlement of disputes, actions against crime, and so forth. It is estimated that about twenty-five per cent of South African voters live under and accept traditional rule, primarily in rural areas, although the migrant labour system brought traditionalism into urban areas. To the extent that one can talk about inter-ethnic violence, it is found in the mines among migrant workers who are still bound to a traditional lifestyle.

Any political party or leader who wants to tackle or undermine traditionalism from within a liberal-democratic constitution can bet on instability for South Africa.

Although traditionalism must be accommodated in order to achieve stability, it is clearly a question of undemocratic stability. Mangosuthu Buthelezi was democratically elected from within Inkatha, but he is also a traditional leader. Democratic and traditional leadership are reconciled in his person. His access to and support from traditional Zulu culture make him a formidable political leader. His influence is disproportionate to the democratic support he enjoys and he is uniquely accommodated within the democratic dispensation, precisely because he has the traditional power base to disrupt it. The local government elections of 2000 will no doubt highlight the tension between political traditionalism and modernity.

If I had to identify two external sources of potential instability, they would be globalisation and regional conflict. Globalisation refers to the greater mobility and transferability of capital, technology, information and skills. At the end of the twentieth century it was perhaps the dominant international tendency, over which no country or person has any control. If you have transferable skills or capital, globalisation is an exciting challenge that invites you to become a citizen of the world without considering national borders or citizenship. In fact, it is argued that globalisation is a frontal attack on the autonomy of the nation state, and there are commentators who say that the time of the nation state is over. On the other hand, it must be borne in mind that if you are uneducated or unemployed, globalisation is a threat. You have no transferable capital or skills and are completely dependent on the nation state for basic services and support. Therefore it can be said that the more prosperous and technologically developed a country is, the less important the nation state is to its citizens and the more globalisation is welcomed.

Conversely, the poorer and less developed a country is, the greater is the dependence on the nation state and the more problematic the impact of globalisation. The South African government has no other choice than to be a part of globalisation. The measures it chooses to make this happen can, in the short term, cause hardship for its poorer citizens. If too many concessions are made to the poor – for example, through labour legislation, health services, and so on – the wealthy feel threatened and tend to use their skills and capital to emigrate. In this sense globalisation can be a source of political instability and a loss of expertise, and it can further contribute to the weakening of the nation state.

Analysts point out that South Africa is suffering from a weak neighbourhood effect. In other words, most neighbouring countries are considerably poorer and less economically developed than South Africa. As a result there is a disproportionate inflow of citizens from other African countries to South Africa, which places an additional burden on the state to deliver efficient services. One can summarise this by saying that the greater the political instability and unemployment in a neighbouring country, the more attractive South Africa becomes.

When a protracted regional war or conflict takes place, as has been the case in the Democratic Republic of the Congo and Angola, this dilemma is heightened dramatically. These wars have already involved six countries and place a huge economic strain on them. What should South Africa do? It is in her interest to foster peace at a regional level, but how should this be achieved? Diplomacy has its limitations. A military peace force costs money. And yet, if nothing is done and the conflict worsens, it has the potential to destabilise all surrounding states. Southern Africa could be saddled with a refugee population that migrates from country to country in order to survive and find shelter.

But after noting all the qualifications that sterilise analyses of possible mistakes, one question emerges which grips the imagination: what would you do if you were in Thabo Mbeki's shoes? This question cuts across the boundary between analysis and practice. A practical decision has practical consequences; an analytical assumption merely shifts the debate to a new discussion.

Naturally the question can never be answered satisfactorily, for two main reasons: you can never be Thabo Mbeki and you will, therefore, not be in a position of power where your decisions would have practical consequences. The closest you can get would be to conduct a 'what if' analysis by pretending you are Thabo Mbeki, but this could become an intellectual game. It seems to me that the only meaningful way to address the problem is *not* to pretend that you are Thabo Mbeki but to say: if my analysis of tendencies and dilemmas is valid, what is Thabo Mbeki *doing* that indicates he is taking them into account? It is, of course, just another analysis, but nevertheless an analysis of his behaviour and the consequences that may flow from it. At this level of analysis the personal, intimate dimension is not of primary importance. I am not saying that it plays no role, but that the role is not significant. That is why I am not terribly interested in Thabo Mbeki's personal choices, primordial urges or fleeting personal transgressions. What interests me is whether he behaves rationally in terms of the central dilemma I have identified and how he manages it. The answer to this question gives me greater insight into what could happen to South Africa rather than what will happen to Thabo Mbeki personally.

What is the central political dilemma? How does President Thabo Mbeki achieve stability within the framework of a liberal democracy in South Africa, especially when he has to manage the political pain of inevitable economic transformation? I know of no other person in the ANC leadership who understands this dilemma better than he does. His personal intellectual development did not make him an enthusiastic supporter of a free market economy and a liberal democracy. He did, however, understand the importance of both after the fall of organised communism in 1989.

My experience of the ANC in exile at various meetings, courses and conferences between 1986 and 1989 was that a liberal-democratic constitution and an economic policy based on free market principles were the last things they had in mind for South Africa. One speaker after the other, including Mbeki, Alec Erwin, Pallo Jordan, Mac Maharaj and Essop Pahad, repeatedly referred to the tension and hardship that the pursuit of both would create in the current South African dispensation. It is precisely this tension and hardship that are creating problems for the ANC in power and which threaten stability. If the ANC makes too many concessions to the poor and unemployed through policies of freewheeling socialism and uncontrolled spending, capital flows out, inflation rockets and there is political instability. Conversely, if the ANC makes too many concessions to the imperatives of a market economy through monetary and fiscal discipline, it creates short-term hardship among the poor, the unemployed and organised labour, which primarily affects the ANC vote, and it becomes a source of political instability. What should Mbeki do?

His first priority is to gain control. Not over the Constitution; this he has in any case with a clear majority, two-thirds or not. He would be unwise to use a two-thirds majority to suspend the Constitution. A liberal-democratic constitution is, in fact, seen internationally as part of his solution and not part of his problem. In any case, historically speaking, very few constitutions have been suspended by means of a two-thirds majority. Germany under Hitler was an exception. Usually a constitution is suspended if a government runs the risk of losing democratically (for example, when General Sani Abacha refused to accept Chief Moshood Abiola as the democratically elected head of state of Nigeria) or when interest groups rise up and carry out a *coup d'état* (as was the case in Chile in 1973).

Mbeki must gain control over two things primarily: the ANC and the policy-making process. The one is related to the other. Under Nelson Mandela there was too much charisma and too little governance, and the person of Mandela was vital in helping South Africa through its first stages of transition. Mbeki knows he has less charisma and he is aiming for more governance. How does he gain control over the ANC? By determining who the public representatives and key executive officials will be. This is happening in a determined and systematic manner. The Deployment Committee of the National Executive Committee determines who seventy-five per cent of the public representatives at central and provincial level will be, and it approves *all* provincial premiers. The appointment of directors-general of state departments and other key officials – for example, at the Reserve Bank – is taking place on an ongoing basis. A widespread system of patronage is being established. The propaganda culture is one of 'discipline and unity of the ANC', but in reality it is about loyalty to Mbeki and his policies.

How does he gain control of policy? This has already begun. The Presidential Review Commission's report was presented in 1998. It was damning of Mandela's administration and policy-making: the lack of co-ordination between essential departments, unsystematic and eclectic policy formulation, sluggishness in acting against corruption, disorganisation in the office of the president, and so forth. Mandela conceded most of these and asked for understanding of the fact that the ANC 'came out of the bush and prison to govern'. One of the recommendations Cabinet accepted was that a co-ordinating and implementing unit be created and that it be based in the office of then deputy president Thabo Mbeki. It started with nine posts and by the time the 2 June 1999 elections took place, there were a hundred and thirty. Five months into Mbeki's presidency it had a staff of three hundred and thirty, had a budget of R70 million and had become part of the presidency.

The task of this unit is, from within the office of the president, to co-ordinate policy and interaction between the Cabinet and the office of the president, between cabinet committees and the office of the president, between state departments, and between them and the office of the president. The organisational structure is strongly reminiscent of the management style of P.W. Botha. In this sense the old lives on in the new. But what is new are the goals that have to be co-ordinated and the circumstances under which this must take place. In the old dispensation it was about the stability of a security system under which a minority's interests were to be controlled undemocratically. In the new, it is about reconciling opposing demands within a democratic constitution in the interests of political stability. Mention has already been made of the conflicting demands between economic growth and democratic participation, human rights and law and order, fiscal discipline and service delivery, traditionalism and modernity. Coping with these demands and smoothing over difficulties will pose a huge challenge to Mbeki's political ingenuity and that is why the country will increasingly be governed from his office. It is still too early to reach a conclusion about how successful and efficient the presidency is, but the intentions are clear.

Does it matter? Let us imagine that under Mbeki's rule there is strong economic growth, stronger law and order, more systematic service delivery and traditional leaders who co-operate to achieve stability. Who is going to complain that there is too little democracy? But if we imagine that under Mbeki's rule a market economy is sacrificed in favour of democratic participation, law and order is consistently sacrificed to an uncritical obsession with human rights, service delivery takes place without consideration of fiscal discipline, and traditional leaders rebel because their authority is being undermined, the question is: who is going to manage the inevitable instability? And how?

When Mbeki took over as president, he knew with relative certainty that the internal 'liberated' ANC had been stabilised, the United Democratic Front was 'dead', competing leadership (Cyril Ramaphosa, Mathews Phosa, Chris Hani) had been neutralised or had died, the 'island group' had retired or had left politics, and potential recalcitrants (Winnie Mandela, Mosiuoa Lekota, Mbhazima Shilowa) had been co-opted. At the same time he has control over who says anything on behalf of the ANC and what that is. In other words, he is as in control as he can be. Now he must begin to govern.

These thoughts occupied me on the morning of 16 June 1999 while I, along with thousands of other people, waited in the amphitheatre of the Union Buildings for

Thabo Mbeki to be inaugurated as the second democratically elected president of the Republic of South Africa. Compared with the inauguration of Mandela in 1994, there was a totally different atmosphere. Then it was a change of regime; this time it was a succession. One could see it in the composition of the audience. In 1994 the previous establishment was clearly present and one could feel the tension. In 1999 it was virtually absent. Pik Botha was there, looking somewhat lost. De Klerk was not – he was marketing his autobiography overseas. Not that anyone really noticed. The atmosphere was relaxed and genial.

Mbeki's inauguration speech was not impressive. Too forcedly profound and delivered in the sonorous cadences and chanting style of an Anglican priest. On top of that he had a sore throat and the Boeings flew over just as he came to the most important point. At the banquet that evening, Mandela upstaged him with humour and charm.

But with the start of the parliamentary sitting two weeks later it was a different story. Mbeki had announced his Cabinet earlier that week and it reflected his confidence and control. Two of his exile confidants, Penuell Maduna and Steve Tshwete, are helping him to uphold law and order. His opening speech was by far the best I have ever heard in a South African Parliament. He has a thorough intellectual grip on the problems facing the country: crime, investment, education, corruption and effective administration. There was not much with which the opposition could find fault. They clung to the Mahlangu incident like manna from heaven throughout the no-confidence debate.

Mbeki had appointed Ndaweni Mahlangu as premier of Mpumalanga and had kicked Mathews Phosa out. Mahlangu held a press conference at which he explained why he had re-appointed two former provincial cabinet members who had been fired by the former administration on suspicion of corruption. With astonishing naïveté, Mahlangu said that most politicians lied and that it was not such a terrible thing. This, just after Mbeki had committed himself, earnestly and categorically, to an honest and clean administration. Everyone waited for his reply in the no-confidence debate.

It was an unhappy performance. He came across as arrogant, snide and intolerant, and refused to address the merits of the case. The press did not spare him and repeatedly threw his own words back at him. Had I not known him so well, I would have been filled with disappointment. The man is just too intelligent and astute to get bogged down in such banality. He still enjoys the benefit of my doubt, but it was not a pleasant start to his first parliamentary session.

Mbeki's shrewdness can be seen in the way he has co-opted possible opponents and involved them in policy implementation. Paradoxical as it might seem, the free market system in South Africa is currently being protected and developed by communists. Alec Erwin, minister of trade and industry, Geraldine Fraser-Moleketi, minister of public service and administration (and beleaguered with labour unrest in the civil service), Jeff Radebe, minister of state enterprises (responsible for privatisation), and Mbhazima Shilowa, who as Gauteng premier must administer the richest province in the country and develop it economically, are all high-ranking members of the SACP. If one had asked financial experts in 1990 what the value of the rand would be under these circumstances, it is not difficult to imagine what their answer would have been.

I often wonder silently whether it is possible to predict

accurately what will happen on a socio-economic and political level. Just imagine if Ronald Reagan and Mikhail Gorbachev had not made peace, if P.W. Botha had not had his stroke and was still in power, if the Berlin Wall had not fallen in 1989, if Oliver Tambo had returned hale and hearty from exile and had not been paralysed by a stroke, if Chris Hani were still alive – in what kind of country would we be living now? To me the journey from Dakar to a democracy in South Africa was one without maps or road signs. It is only with hindsight that one can become so clever.

8 Truth without Reconciliation, Reconciliation without Truth

IT IS 10 MAY 1994, a sunny autumn morning at the amphitheatre of the Union Buildings in Pretoria. Along with thousands of other people I wait for the inauguration of Nelson Mandela as the first democratically elected president of South Africa. I am still light-headed with disbelief at the pace with which national reconciliation has taken place since F.W. de Klerk delivered his epoch-making speech on 2 February 1990 in the Parliament of the old South Africa.

Immediately thereafter De Klerk called together all the traditional Afrikaner organisations – the churches, the cultural organisations, the Broederbond – and for three days they deliberated upon the best way forward and how to create a climate which could reduce the tension and uncertainty. Their declaration showed the necessity to work together for a common future and to try systematically to get to know the ANC and all other struggle organisations better. The rightwing groups made it clear that they wanted nothing to do with these changes, and some of the more militant struggle groups agitated for an intensification of the armed struggle.

When Mandela came out of jail he went straight to the Cape Town Parade. In his impromptu speech he emphasised that it was a dangerous time for the country. The fears and mistrust of the past were still with us. He took the hand De Klerk held out to him and said they, and all of us, had to begin working on national reconciliation.

Shortly afterwards, they jointly formed a reconciliation committee comprising political, church and business leaders, and produced a plan of action. The idea was to establish similar committees at local government level, in schools and universities and nongovernmental organisations. The aim of all these reconciliation committees was for people to speak directly and frankly about the past so that as many people as possible would be informed about what had happened, with the aim of ensuring that these mistakes would never be made again.

The thorny issue of accountability for serious crimes against human rights had to be settled. Mandela and De Klerk called an amnesty congress at which the senior officers of security forces on all sides, selected lawyers, church leaders and representatives of Spain, Chile, Argentina, Uruguay and Germany were present. These are all countries that had to make peace with a divisive, traumatic past. For three days there were serious and frank discussions about who did what and who took which decisions. The whole debate happened in public, with national and international television coverage. The final session was held *in camera*, and it produced an amnesty declaration. There would be collective amnesty for all, but where there was *prima facie* evidence of individual responsibility for misdeeds, justice had to take its course. After sentencing, a personal amnesty could be considered. This was not an ideal state of affairs, but everyone agreed that it was more important to work towards a common future than to continually dwell upon a fractured past. At the press conference Mandela took De Klerk's hand and said, 'We must forgive but never forget.'

Mandela worked tirelessly with rightwing groups to draw them into the process of reconciliation. Eventually first Carel Boshoff, then Constand Viljoen committed to the process. Doing so isolated fanatics such as Eugene Terre'Blanche and his followers, and considerably reduced the possibility of violence. Both De Klerk and Mandela worked to stabilise the situation between Inkatha and the ANC and to stop the violence in Natal. Eventually Mangosuthu Buthelezi could see that there was also space for him in the new South Africa. In the meantime the negotiating process for an interim constitution progressed relatively smoothly and it was decided to set up a government of national unity for five years, to hold a democratic general election, and that the top structures of the civil service, except in extreme cases of irresponsibility, would remain unchanged for the five-year term, with the instruction that they shared their knowledge with their potential successors during that period. As far as possible, affirmative action would be reconciled with knowledge and competence. The civil service and the private sector committed themselves to making as much knowledge and training as possible available to the new democratic government during this transitional process.

The elections went by peacefully and effectively, and here we all are now, sitting at the Union Buildings, waiting for the inauguration ceremony to begin. There is an underlying optimism and excitement in all of us. The reconciliation process has exceeded everybody's wildest hopes. It could have been a hundred times worse. Who will ever forget how Mandela and De Klerk hugged each other at the ceremony where each received the Nobel Prize for peace? There was not a dry eye here or in the rest of the world.

Mandela is sworn in and starts speaking. He talks about the time before and after his liberation; about the process of reconciliation to date. It is stirring, raw and sincere. There is a deathly silence. He ends, 'I now say in front of all of you and the whole world: the greater part of my productive life was destroyed by an inhuman system that was maintained by our fellow citizens. It caused immeasurable pain and suffering. But if I look at where we are now and the promises that the future holds for all of us, then I have no hesitation in saying to F.W. de Klerk and his people: what I and my people suffered under your party's rule we will never forget, but we forgive you, and I invite you, and them, to build a new country with us.'

Mandela holds out his hand to De Klerk. De Klerk gets up, takes the hand offered to him and they look each other in the eye while there is tumultuous applause all round. Eventually De Klerk gets the chance to say something. 'Mister President, you have pre-empted me. Before you can forgive me, I must confess so that you and the world will know what I am asking forgiveness for. I entered the politics of our country with verve and enthusiasm because I, and so many of my fellow party members, believed in the rightness of what we were trying to do. Gradually I began to realise that what we wanted to do could not be implemented and had no justifiable moral foundation. When I became state president this realisation became even stronger. That is why I made the speech of 2 February, which marked the beginning of the process that has brought us here today. But, Mister President, never in my wildest dreams did I imagine the extent of the harm and pain our policies had caused. My colleagues and I dismissed those who tried to make us aware of this as propagandists with hidden agendas. It was the reconciliation process, which you and I initiated, that opened my eyes. Together we travelled across the country and I heard first-hand how people had suffered under our policies and security laws. I did not want to believe what I heard coming out of the De Kock hearings. But I say to you now and to the whole world: De Kock was right. He and so many like him could not have acted in isolation. We who governed made it possible. It is no use to claim that we did not know. We did not want to know, and if we knew, we did nothing about it. There can be no reconciliation without forgiveness. But there can also be no forgiveness without confession.

'I want to confess today on behalf of my people and myself, before you and the world, that we were fundamentally and completely wrong. That we almost wreaked irreversible damage on our country and its people. For that I ask your forgiveness and that of your people. I also beg forgiveness for your personal suffering. But, Mister President, my people and I do not just need the forgiveness of you and your people. I also ask forgiveness from the young people who died unnecessarily for an indefensible cause, and especially from their parents. I also ask forgiveness from the thousands of officials we pumped full of a false patriotic duty to implement an impossible policy. Especially, I ask forgiveness of the security staff in the police and army who had to stand at the forefront of oppression. We misled them horribly. Yes, I even ask forgiveness of De Kock, that we made it possible for him to become what he became.

'Mister President, if the forgiveness you offer me also allows for my confession, then I again take the hand you have held out to me and I say to you: let us begin rebuilding this torn country of ours together.'

Mandela and De Klerk embrace each other once again in front of the whole world. Again there is not a dry eye here or anywhere else in the world.

As Gagiano would say, 'I dreamt I was awake when it all happened.' But of course I am awake and it was all just a dream. To bring truth and reconciliation together in our country would at the very least require a process on this scale. Reconciliation on such a collective and social scale has to work by means of an awe-inspiring power of example, a cleansing ritual loaded with the symbolism of atonement–forgiveness–reconciliation. The truth referred to here is not the truth of the law and science, but the truth that comes from confiding and acknowledging, a sort of confessional truth. There is no guarantee that if it happens, there will inevitably be reconciliation. But at least at a leadership level the example of personal reconciliation needs to be made. If there is mistrust, estrangement and a lack of confession and forgiveness here, how on God's earth can a general climate of reconciliation be fostered? In both De Klerk's and Mandela's autobiographies it becomes clear that their relationship systematically deteriorated. After reading De Klerk's autobiography I was filled with revulsion. There is not the faintest trace of personal accountability for what happened in this country under his party's rule. Instead there are excuses and self-glorification. He is the born reformer who knew from the beginning what had to happen. At the Nobel Prize ceremony De Klerk and Mandela could barely hide their contempt for each other. Mandela's willingness to forgive was never reciprocated by De Klerk's confession. On the contrary, De Klerk behaved as if forgiveness was his due.

That is why the Truth and Reconciliation Commission (TRC) was doomed from the start to an uphill battle as an instrument of national reconciliation. In fact, if anything made it clear that my dream was totally unrealistic, it was the reality exposed by the TRC process. The indescribable cruelty, torture, pain, confusion and senseless suffering experienced by the victims was never, other than in highly exceptional instances, answered with confession and accountability. One got the impression that the few who did come to confess had no other choice because the evidence that had emerged from the De Kock hearings was so damning against them. And even when some of them came to testify, the grey safari suit and shoes tucked away for the occasion, they still tried to evade, conveniently forgot, and transferred responsibility. The general impression they created was that they genuinely could not understand why *they* were the ones who had to come forward. They had merely done their duty; they had only been the foot soldiers of the policy-makers.

And the policy-makers were beyond revolting. The senile arrogance of Botha who told the whole TRC process to get stuffed; F.W. de Klerk, legalistic, small-minded and trying to be clever: of course there were gross violations and he did not feel happy about them, but he knew nothing about them personally and never took such decisions. Do the people who sat in the Vorster, Botha and De Klerk cabinets really expect us and the world to believe they took no decisions responsible for the misery? Or that they knew absolutely nothing about it? This after decades of anti-apartheid struggle, murders, court cases, petitions, and so on? Even if they did not accept the TRC as a valid or useful instrument for reconciliation, was there any indication from them that there was a relationship between confession and reconciliation, that reconciliation without confession was not possible?

The response is usually that they were involved in an anti-communist struggle, and that it was not a game for the faint-hearted. But the Total Onslaught strategy only reached maturity later, under Botha. By then the policies of apartheid had been mercilessly implemented for over thirty years. In fact, it was the implementation of this policy that required a Total Strategy against a Total Onslaught. The pass laws, the Group Areas Act, the homeland policies, the law on separate amenities. The consequences of these policies were repeatedly spelt out in South Africa and abroad through research, conferences, seminars, protests, and so forth. This is the policy that shaped the interdependent process of liberation and oppression. A process in which success was defined as the destruction of the other.

So the climate was created in which all sides were guilty of cruelty. A necklace murder cannot be separated from the murder of an MK soldier. Winnie Mandela who glared at Desmond Tutu with fixed, bitter eyes while he begged her to say that she felt just a little bit sorry. Her entire attitude said, 'Stompie was a traitor, he betrayed the struggle. The struggle was the fight against apartheid. It was a holy fight. Can't the meddlesome priest understand this?'

When De Klerk delivered his 2 February speech, my very first reaction was: do he and the NP really understand what they have unleashed here? Coincidentally I had, from Oxford, spoken to him on the phone the week before. A business associate, Dick Enthoven, had seen him in Johannesburg. They had started talking and from the discussion Dick had got the impression that De Klerk would like to talk to me. I asked Dick why. He was vague and uncertain but said De Klerk had given him a contact number. Because I was due back in South Africa for a short break from Oxford, I phoned De Klerk. He was quite friendly and amiable but I could not figure out what he wanted to talk about. When I told him I was coming to South Africa, he said I should visit him if I had the chance, but not before 2 February. According to him there was going to be a 'little acceleration' in policy.

Imagine that: the end of apartheid and the start of negotiations for a completely democratic alternative was 'an acceleration' of policy! When I met De Klerk in his office after 2 February and asked him why he had made the speech, his answer was that he had, on the one hand, experienced a 'spiritual leap' away from apartheid and, on the other hand, that he would have been crazy not to take the gap presented by the fall of communism in Eastern Europe.

I left the meeting with the distinct impression that he did not really understand the implications of what he had done, and especially that he was convinced he could control the process throughout. He was completely unaware of the problems that lay ahead, particularly at a security level. When I took my leave of him I commented that he had inherited a difficult security situation. He was somewhat surprised. 'Do you really think so?' he asked.

The one thing the TRC demonstrated clearly was that De Klerk, the NP and the security forces were totally unprepared for the moral and ethical implications of the dismantling of apartheid, and that, if it were to lead to national reconciliation, it would require creative political actions from them all. De Klerk had no remorse and seemed to be offended, as if South Africa and the world could not appreciate the greatness of his deed (and it was indeed great); the NP was totally confused and unprepared; and the security forces were furious about the betrayal and deceit practised upon them. They were especially upset because the politicians pretended they had been totally unaware of the work the security forces had had to do at the coal-face of oppression to keep the system alive. It was this work, exposed by the TRC, that filled good, loyal supporters of the NP with shame, and persuaded many of them to confess their unknowing accountability. But not De Klerk and his buddies.

I do not for one moment want to suggest that the ANC or other struggle organisations were all a bunch of innocent, naïve victims. Testimony was also given of gruesome deeds and cruelty on their part. Variations of the 'just war' philosophy were also produced, which sometimes sounded strange, and examples of sanctimonious struggle piety were plentiful. But the example set by Mandela, whatever his personal feelings, was one of unqualified reconciliation. From his visit to Betsie Verwoerd, his actions at the 1995 Rugby World Cup final, and his negotiations with Constand Viljoen, up to his many speeches immediately after liberation and his inauguration on 10 May 1994, it was clear that he wanted reconciliation. He repeatedly stated his willingness to forgive the past. This example influenced his followers and I do not doubt for a moment that it played a crucial role in the smooth unfolding of the first five years. But the example of a willingness to forgive on the one hand, without confession on the other, makes national reconciliation almost impossible.

Against this background it is valid to ask whether the TRC was the most suitable instrument to achieve the goal. Before answering this question I want to state categorically that Alex Boraine is a very good friend. He is not the first friend with whom I have differed fundamentally on an issue but who still remains a friend. Boraine was primarily responsible for the legislation that eventually resulted in the establishment of the TRC and he later became deputy chairman of the TRC. Now that the most important tasks of the TRC have been completed, both he and Tutu, who was chairman, are lecturing in the United States. The world, especially the United States, is much more fascinated and impressed by the TRC than people in South Africa are – a case of the prophet not being honoured in his own country. Alex is currently a visiting professor of transitional justice at the University of New York. (These Americans!) I tease him, and tell him it is time he came round to permanent justice. In any case, long before, during and after the TRC hearings I argued with him and with people close to the TRC. The following are the points I regard as becoming most important.

The TRC is based on suppositions and assumptions that, even if they are not demonstrably invalid, are nevertheless misleading and ambiguous. What is the notion of truth assumed here? It must be universal and transferable, otherwise the entire process is senseless. By definition it cannot be a relativistic truth because, as someone once said, 'If someone tells you there is no such thing as truth, he is asking you not to believe him. Don't.' That is why you cannot have your truth and I mine if we want the same reconciliation. We must at least agree that we are referring to the same truth for which confession, forgiveness and reconciliation are being asked, otherwise it could become quite a mess. So how do we get to this truth? Here, it is not about verifiable scientific truth in the pure sense of the word. In a traditional society, truth is determined by the priests, a king, a captain or group leaders. In modern industrial societies, the truth of accountability is determined by the country's prevailing justice system. The fact that we speak of an international tribunal of justice assumes that on an international level there exists such a generally acceptable process of cross-examination, defence and delivery of testimony, and that the judgement of the court is accepted as valid and true. If there are reasonable grounds for doubt, the right to appeal is granted. In other words, the truth of accountability is determined through law. This is the closest that we sorry sinners can get to the truth.

Now the TRC comes along and says that it will determine truth without legal process. How will it do this? By giving people the opportunity to recount the terrible things that happened to them, and giving others the chance to tell how they did those terrible things, and then to ensure that there is reconciliation between them? Let me concede immediately that something rings very true in a confession. When someone says, 'I am sorry, I did it,' ninety-nine per cent of the time we are prepared to believe such a person. (Even then they are sometimes lying.) But what do you do when people do not want to confess? If you have reasonable grounds for believing that the person is guilty, you take him or her to court. The TRC expressly states that it is not a court, however. It has the right to summons people to appear before it, but it cannot, through ordinary legal process, cross-examine people in order to determine accountable truth. If it wished to be this type of court, it would have had to become a special court for specific purposes of the prevailing justice system. But then the TRC would never have fulfilled its mandate within the given timeframe and court cases would continue for several years.

Because the TRC cannot force accountable truth by means of confession, it becomes a sort of quasi-court where those summonsed or volunteering to appear are confronted with a mass of circumstantial evidence and an implication of guilt, which cannot, however, be proved by means of legal process. This causes everyone listening or watching to think: the bastard is guilty. Whether it be Winnie Mandela, De Klerk, P.W. Botha or the leader of a defence unit, their instinctive reaction is, 'Go to hell.' The victims become embittered, the suspects become embittered, and both question the validity and usefulness of the TRC. The only exceptions are those individuals who were almost forced to make a confession because they were revealed through normal legal process as people with an obvious burden of guilt. For example, Biko's murderers as a result of the De Kock hearings. There they were, pathetic in their evasive admissions. Benzien was an exception. In front of the TRC, crying, he sat on someone's back to demonstrate how he had tried to smother Tony Yengeni. Yengeni sat there, listening to him. Nobody doubted for a moment that Benzien was telling the truth.

But what about reconciliation? The assumption is that truth leads to reconciliation. But this is demonstrably rubbish. The divorce courts prove this every day. Biko's widow made it crystal-clear in front of the TRC, and I have great understanding for her point of view. There stood the murderers of her husband, shameless in their lack of remorse, trying to obtain amnesty on technical grounds. Why should she forgive them, even if they were telling the truth? But, it can be argued, the truth is at least a precondition for reconciliation. Again, evidence for this is of doubtful value. There are plenty of examples showing that legally, technical accountable truth has led to revenge, hatred and retribution. But what about confessed truth? The chances are better, but there is no guarantee that this is either necessary or sufficient. The assumption that truth leads to reconciliation or that it is a necessary prerequisite is based on sentimental theological assumptions that very often bear no relation to reality.

Can there be reconciliation without truth? Of course there can. Often truth is the first victim of reconciliation. Many married couples are reconciled precisely because the parties do not want to know or hear about the past. Is this real reconciliation? What, in fact, is real reconciliation? It is a relationship that is restored to the extent that the parties can move on in peace while accepting each other's integrity. If this had happened collectively in South Africa, we would be winning now. In Spain, a formal decision was taken not to speak about the past. To what extent is Spain a non-reconciled country? In Chile it was decided to grant a general amnesty without accountability. What evidence exists that if Chile, like South Africa, had tried to establish accountable amnesty outside the process of law, it would be a better-reconciled country today? The only available evidence is South Africa itself. Is it a reconciled country? Read Antjie Krog's *Country of My Skull*, Jacques Pauw's *Prime Evil* and think of Max du Preez's television programmes about the TRC and the answer is evident. But simply the way the TRC report was received is indication enough. F.W. de Klerk and Constand Viljoen saw the whole process as retribution by the ANC and, in the case of De Klerk, also as a personal vendetta on the part of Alex Boraine. Mbeki sought a court order against the release of the report because it placed apartheid and the struggle on the same moral level. After the report had been tabled, Tutu and Boraine left the country. There are no follow-ups to consolidate the reconciliation facilitated by the TRC. In fact, what reconciliation? The impression is rather that everyone would like to forget the whole affair as quickly as possible.

But what about guilt? How far should it stretch? Is guilt possible without accountability? If I did not know, should I have known? If I knew but did nothing, am I accountable for the murders that took place, for the suffering under apartheid? What about the fact that I was an unknowing beneficiary of apartheid? To whom should I confess? From whom should I ask forgiveness for what I did not know, but from which I nevertheless benefited? And if I was aware but was too scared to do anything about it, how can I now rectify something I did not do? There are an infinite number of possible answers to these questions. One could start with the 'original sin' entrepreneurs: the theologians and priests who know what is going on in God's head. We were all born and received in sin. That may well be, but it will not help us get to Biko's murderers. Then one could start with the social philosophers who will say that the real guilt should be at the door of colonialism, capitalism, nationalism, communism, socialism, and so forth. Once again that may be true, but it will not help us get to Biko's murderers either. Mahmood Mamdani, the anthropologist, becomes very agitated because the TRC process allowed the great majority of those privileged under apartheid to get away scot-free. He has a point, but what mechanism does he suggest to address collective guilt? Expropriation of property? A once-off tax? But this has everything to do with retribution and nothing at all to do with reconciliation. Can one build a better future through retribution than through successful reconciliation without truth? I do not know.

What I do know is that there are only two means of arriving at the truth in a social context: one is through the legal process and the other through personal confession. And I can lie even when I confess. Whether both are needed or just one is sufficient for reconciliation is an empirical question that cannot be predetermined by means of simplistic assumptions of a romanticised, sentimental morality.

Does this mean we should not be interested in the truth about our past? Of course not. That truth will be exposed to us through research, drama, literature, journalism and film. This is the great value of the work of Krog, Pauw, Du Preez and so many others. And also of the TRC process. Nobody can remain unmoved by the terrible deeds exposed by that process. Hopefully, through it we will learn to avoid similar horrific deeds in future. Probably we will find that the truth about the past holds infinitely more lessons for us than were exposed by the TRC.

And what about reconciliation? It is absolutely necessary if we want this country to turn the corner. But it will probably take many years, if not decades, before it becomes meaningful to all of us in our daily lives. If the political leadership does not want to set the example, the TRC and the courts will not be able to do it. The 1999 election campaign was also not too encouraging in this regard. Perhaps we will have to privatise the reconciliation process.

I know the TRC was established with the best intentions. I debated the issue at length with Boraine. Cultural philosopher Isaiah Berlin used an Emmanuel Kant phrase for the title of one of his works: 'Out of the crooked timber of humanity, nothing straight was ever born.' He made the point that the cult of sincerity is one of the curses of the twentieth century. It is quite simply not good enough. You can be sincere and stupid, sincere and uninformed, sincere and ignorant, sincere and incompetent. All we can hope for is that we are sincere enough to admit our mistakes and to avoid them in future. Nothing is more dangerous than a dogmatic and sincere ideologue.

Was the entire TRC process a failure? Yes, if one wanted to bring truth and reconciliation together. No, if it made us all aware of where we come from and the direction in which we must move. What is its usefulness to today's politics? I think all the parties concerned want to get away from the TRC as quickly as possible. My information, which comes from the former president's office, is that from the outset the new government was never very keen on the TRC. The ANC was always in favour of a general amnesty and a fresh start. It was the NP that prevented this. My nose tells me that, to sustain peace in KwaZulu-

Natal and accommodate the former generals, Mbeki's government will sooner rather than later find a means of circumventing the amnesty terms of the TRC. Then, with or without the TRC, we will have to start working on reconciliation. In any event, it is going to be an uphill battle.

Epilogue: The Here and Now

EVEN THOUGH I HAVE BEEN without party affiliations and out of parliamentary politics for almost fourteen years, the most common question I am asked is: 'When are you coming back to politics?' There are two misconceptions hidden in the question. One is that you can only be involved in politics if you are a member of a party in Parliament. The other is that politics is something static, like the Voortrekker Monument, that you can visit and leave according to whim.

The Parliament I left can in almost no way be compared to the Parliament that exists today. In the intervening time I was perhaps more politically involved than when I was a member of Parliament. The composition and nature of party politics and the points of conflict that separate parties today cannot be compared with what went before. The sociopolitical context in which the previous Parliament functioned and that in which the new one operates differ dramatically. Sometimes I get the impression that the Democratic Party does not appreciate this: parliamentary ritual can continue unhindered as before, with perhaps a slight change of gear.

During the old dispensation Louis Luyt asked me one day to meet him. This was after I had left Parliament. He said the country was heading for disaster and the time had come to create a new, unified opposition party. He wanted me to lead the party, which was to be named the Democratic Party (DP). At that stage, Zach de Beer, Wynand

Malan and Denis Worrall were all leaders of small opposition parties, with Zach de Beer's Progressive Federal Party being the largest. I suggested to Louis that, although I felt his instinct was right, launching a party was not quite the same as blowing a whistle and ordering a scrum. In any case, I was too busy with IDASA and extra-parliamentary politics to be interested in something like this.

A few weeks later the DP was launched with a troika leadership, namely De Beer, Worrall and Malan. That did not last long and De Beer won the tussle for leadership. Colin Eglin is by far the best politician in the DP, but he was overlooked. In the new order, Tony Leon is leader of the DP and this party became the official opposition after the general elections of 1999. De Beer has passed away, Worrall is a businessman and Malan is a commissioner for the Truth and Reconciliation Commission. Leon is undoubtedly both clever and articulate. I get the impression he would have been an excellent Tory in the British parliament. His style is pure Westminster.

About two months before the 1999 elections I was part of a discussion which could have led to my becoming involved in party politics again. Leon and Lawrence Schlemmer, a gifted social researcher and an old friend, were having dinner at my house. We were discussing the forthcoming elections and possible trends. To me the only possible new dynamic lay in the election battle in the Western Cape. Even though the New National Party (NNP) had become the ruling party in the province after the 1994 elections, De Klerk's withdrawal from the government of national unity and his resignation as leader of the NNP had fatally damaged the party. With a strong and well-planned campaign, the DP had an outside chance of becoming the majority party. There was speculation about whether I should become the candidate for premier. I said I might consider it, on condition that, if the DP were successful, it would form a coalition with the ANC.

Both Schlemmer and Leon were strongly opposed to such a move. They felt it would make the DP vulnerable with regard to the NNP in the Western Cape and that it underestimated the anti-ANC sentiments in the province. My feeling was that these considerations were perhaps valid in the short term and for election purposes, but that in the long term they would restrict the opposition, consisting of the DP and the NNP, and that this would only increase racial polarisation. The anti-ANC hysteria was precisely the issue from which one had to move away in order to shift the debate towards the more substantial political problems of the day. The DP should try to win support on the basis of political education rather than play on short-term advantages and fears. The counter-argument was that without significant support one could not play a meaningful educational role. Against this I argued that the way support was mobilised could make an educational role impossible. So the argument twisted and turned. Eventually I made it clear that I did not see a future for myself with the DP. I had in any case been quite lukewarm about the option. This was the last time I was tempted to consider parliamentary politics.

Nevertheless, I was and still am convinced that the Western Cape offered a golden opportunity to develop a new dynamic within parliamentary politics. On election day I ran into Marthinus van Schalkwyk, leader of the NNP, at the Independent Electoral Council's centre shortly before counting started. I asked him how the NNP in the Western Cape was going to perform and he said it was very tight, but that although his party would not attain a clear majority, he was confident that the NNP would be the majority party. This meant that the NNP would hold the lead position in forming a coalition. Van Schalkwyk then asked me what I thought he should do. My advice was that the NNP go into coalition with the ANC. (The DP had already officially announced that it would not consider this option.) Such a coalition would capture the imagination and could play a strong reconciliatory role. Attention would shift away from racial politics and focus on the serious political dilemmas that should be dealt with, including poverty, education, crime and effective administration. Much to my surprise, Van Schalkwyk said it was not a bad idea.

Two days later he phoned me and asked whether my advice had been serious. Once again I assured him I had been. He said he was going to try, but expected to meet considerable resistance from within his party. He was right, and in this sense the DP was too. The anti-ANC feelings had been mobilised too strongly during the election campaign now to be done away with through coalition negotiations. And so the DP–NNP coalition was born. The ANC even made it known that it would rather enter into a coalition with the NNP than consider such a relationship with the DP. If anyone had told me ten years ago that the ANC government would prefer the successors of the party that created apartheid to those of the party that Helen Suzman represented, I would have keeled over in astonishment. A more damning indictment of the decay of parliamentary politics would be difficult to imagine.

What do I mean by a new dynamic? This is a complex problem and difficult choices have to be made. I have already referred to the central political dilemma facing the government, namely how to reduce poverty and provide efficient services. The government wishes to address poverty by means of its macro-economic policy, which is in essence market-friendly. The implementation of this policy will cause hardship, before and if the suffering of the poor and unemployed is reduced. These hardships need to be managed politically, because dissatisfaction with them will manifest politically. Civil service union strikes are but one symptom of this. The central political challenge for government, and the country, is how to manage the threatening instability that is a result of the political pain of economic change. At the same time the government has to try to improve the efficiency of the civil service at all levels in order to improve service delivery. Corruption and crime complicate these problems immeasurably.

The DP, NNP and other opposition parties, with the exception of the Inkatha Freedom Party (IFP), are not part of the debate about these problems, because they give priority to the role of a 'strong opposition' within the formal structure of a liberal parliamentary democracy. And it is their right to do so. Once again it is the difficult moral dilemma of choosing between 'good' competing values. On the one hand, Parliament must be used democratically to address the central political problems of the country – this is government's priority. On the other, Parliament must be used democratically to develop a strong opposition that points out government's faults – this is the current opposition parties' priority.

The problem is, however, that there are no really strong ideological differences between the government and the opposition on fundamental policy issues. The DP and the NNP can use the fact that communists are part of the ANC alliance against the government, but the irony is that the government's market-led economic policy, with which the DP and the NNP largely agree, is being maintained by communist cabinet ministers: Trevor Manual in finance, Alec Erwin in trade and industry, Jeff Radebe in privatisation, Geraldine Fraser-Moleketi in the civil service, and so on. In fact, the differences between Leon and Manuel regarding economic policy are trivial compared to the differences between Manuel and communist heavyweight ideologues like Blade Nzimande and Jeremy Cronin.

Because there are no strong ideological differences between government and opposition parties, parliamentary confrontation has been reduced to problems of integrity, dedication to government policy, the speed and enthusiasm of policy implementation, and basic competence. If one looks at the composition of the parties, it is obvious that it is becoming a debate between privileged minorities in opposition and the underprivileged majority in power. In short, opposition says to government, 'You are too stupid to govern,' and, 'We know how to do things better.' It does not require great imagination to realise that such a situation will deteriorate into distasteful 'old South Africa' racial politics. After the elections the DP and NNP entered into a formal coalition while trying to cannibalise each other at the polls by appealing to the baser instincts of the voter.

I do not for a moment believe that people like Tony Leon, Colin Eglin, Ken Andrew, Dene Smuts, and so on, are racists. But regardless of how genuine their commitment to liberal values is, the structural position in which they find themselves – given the formal logic of a liberal-democratic parliament, the central political challenges facing the government, and the choices that the DP makes to be a 'strong opposition' that 'has guts' and 'fights back' – is putting them into the straitjacket of racial politics. It is to escape this that I proposed a coalition between the ANC and the DP. Personally I have no desire to be in that straitjacket. The issues that stem from it are destructive, short-sighted and distasteful. Time and again the debate is side-tracked to deal with issues that have absolutely no bearing on the problems of the country. Unfortunately this merely reinforces old stereotypes and prejudices. It is with a feeling of resentment that I have to come to the unfortunate conclusion that the issue of race will continue to be a part of our politics for a long time to come.

Two months after the elections, the DP invited me to Arniston to address its caucus at a *bosberaad*. This was as a result of a newspaper article I had written in which I had expressed my misgivings about the DP's election campaign. I was hesitant, but after Leon himself asked me to go, I accepted. I stated all the points of criticism again. My views did not find favour and the reaction confirmed all my misgivings. The DP is in for a difficult time.

It seems that Buthelezi and the IFP have recognised the need for a new dynamic – in co-operation with the ANC, of course. The relationship between the IFP and the ANC between the 1994 and 1999 elections changed dramatically from confrontation politics to coalition politics. In the 1994 election the IFP played the ethnic card with statements such as 'The ANC is anti-Zulu and anti-traditional.' In the 1999 elections there was no sign of this and both parties were determined to preserve the peace. We should not harbour the illusion that the ethnic card will not be played again should the relationship between the IFP and the ANC deteriorate. However, it was a conscious political decision to avoid this. Is it possible for the DP to devise a strategy that would make it more difficult for the ANC government and the DP to play the racial card? It is for this reason that a new dynamic is required. For what it is worth, I voted ANC in the 1999 election.

Another matter of which I am more convinced after the

1999 election is that it is virtually impossible for the interests of cultural minorities to be addressed within the workings of party politics in Parliament. In the course of several discussions with Constand Viljoen I have noticed that he has come to the same conclusion. In spite of our serious differences in the old dispensation I have come to know him as an upright and honourable person in his negotiations about the position of what he terms 'ethnic Afrikaners'. He is, nevertheless, deeply uncomfortable in the world of party politics. It must have been a great disillusionment for him to see the extent to which he had overestimated the loyalty of 'ethnic Afrikaners' to party politics. Many of his voters walked right across to vote for the DP. I hope the DP is aware of the implications this support will have for it in future.

Shortly after the elections Viljoen asked me over a cup of coffee, 'Van Zyl, can you tell me why my people left me and voted for Leon?' I suggested that it was because Leon was tougher towards the ANC. Viljoen answered, 'You're right. One of them told me bluntly, "That Jew fights harder against the kaffirs than you do."'

I have already had my say about birthmarks such as race, ethnicity and gender. What surprises me these days is that the issue of being an Afrikaner will simply not fade from my life. When I resigned from Parliament, Mbeki sent me a personal letter of congratulations in which he called me a 'new Voortrekker'. This felt strange to me. My resignation had nothing to do with a need to lead the 'Afrikaner nation' on to a new path. But Mbeki chose to see me in this political light. It was and still is my conviction that if ethnicity is made the source of party-political participation in a parliamentary system, conflict will remain endemic in the politics of South Africa. In fact, this is precisely what the NP of the old regime achieved. That is why I find the title of De Klerk's autobiography, *The Last Trek*, so pretentious. He would have it appear that he led the Afrikaner people to their last resting place in the new South Africa as the 'new Voortrekker leader' – a teleological masturbation.

It is De Klerk's complete lack of understanding of the structure and workings of a liberal democracy which makes him unfit to lead any cultural minority in that direction – not to mention a racially based Afrikaner minority. All that he achieved was to hand minority rule over peacefully to majority rule. On the surface this is a remarkable achievement, but it in no way addresses the problem of cultural minorities. It just emphasises them.

Nobody writes with greater passion, skill and dedication about the Afrikaner as cultural minority in the new South Africa than Hermann Giliomee. I differ from him on his assertion that the ANC consciously and systematically undermines the minority question or is hostile to it. Personally, I believe that the ANC is just too busy putting out other threatening political fires. But I fully agree with Giliomee that being Afrikaans-speaking, the Afrikaans language and the survival of Afrikaans in the educational arena are facing a crisis of existence.

The advantages of a power monopoly have made privileged Afrikaners vulnerable and ill equipped to stand on their own two feet as a cultural group in the new South Africa. Since the ANC government came into power in 1994 I have been invited to address *Boeredae*, the Ruiterwag, the Afrikaanse Taal- en Kultuurvereniging and smaller Afrikaans discussion groups. Sometimes I have been insulted, sometimes criticised and a few times even praised. The greatest common denominator for some is probably that I can speak Afrikaans; others think that in some strange way I am still an Afrikaner, and they want to know how this can be. What constantly strikes me is their total confusion and lack of direction. The comfortable, established world they viewed as a given has collapsed. They feel themselves increasingly to be strangers in the country they previously regarded as their own. One young farmer at the Ruiterwag meeting outside Pretoria put it thus: 'Doc, I don't know whether I am upset because I did not try to find out what had been going on, or because I believed the bastards so easily. Maybe I just wanted to believe them.' I know the area he comes from. I grew up there and I know how it happened that he was unwittingly and systematically silenced and made ill equipped to face the challenges of the new South Africa.

Even when Mbeki addressed two thousand Broeders in the Pretoria City Hall, the first reaction was not: 'How can we take advantage of the space he is giving us to establish ourselves as a new cultural group and make ourselves useful in the new dispensation?' It was: 'Why doesn't he tell us how to adapt? Tell us what we have to do!' Mbeki cannot do this, even if he wanted to. He simply does not have the time or the means. This is the Afrikaner's own problem, which only he can solve. My guess is that Mbeki will try to cater for Afrikaners outside party politics.

The new dispensation is testing the depth of Afrikaners' identification with Afrikaans cultural issues. Is there a significant will to let Afrikaans survive as a language? On whose part? And how? How many Afrikaans-speakers with transferable skills prefer to settle elsewhere when confronted with the option of staying in South Africa or leaving? At the moment the country is being bled dry because so many professionals are leaving. What is there to entice them to stay? Is the Afrikaans language one possibility?

Why do I concern myself with these questions? I am middle aged, very happily married to an English-speaking woman from Swaziland; my children went to English-medium schools after it became too difficult to be 'Slabbert's children' at Afrikaans-medium primary schools; my son speaks mainly English to me, my daughter Afrikaans. Breyten is married to Yolande; he lives primarily in Spain and Paris. They only speak French to each other and he writes mainly in Afrikaans. Still we are constantly debating these things. Why? The answer can range from the existential to the social and ideological. Existentially, a great deal of my daily consciousness is Afrikaans. My interest in philosophical problems; my memories of the past, of good times and difficult times, are Afrikaans. As I have already said, social typecasting strengthens this existential consciousness. I am quite simply seen as being Afrikaans-speaking; even my closest English-speaking friends try to speak Afrikaans to me. Ideologically I find myself protesting against the levelling, almost Jacobean impact of modernisation and globalisation, the convenient and easy acceptance of the unavoidable imperatives of the market. I can understand Mbeki's fundamental problems in job creation. But is the price to be paid for success at this level necessarily the disappearance of cultural diversity? I believe not. But what can be done about it?

Can we learn something from postcolonial African experiences? In Senegal and the Ivory Coast the official language is French; in Mozambique and Angola, Portuguese; in many others, English. And yet the indigenous languages thrive. In Nigeria there is Yoruba, Hausa and Ibo literature. Is the precondition a commitment to traditionalism? This cannot be. Political scientists Kymlycka and Stephan are both studying the survival of ethnic nationalism in post-industrial societies in Central and Eastern Europe.

In fact, Kymlycka even speaks of a charter of minority rights in contrast with, or complementary to, a charter of human rights, because he believes the position of minorities will be one of the greatest challenges for liberal democratic state systems in the twenty-first century.

The annual Afrikaans cultural festivals in Oudtshoorn and Potchefstroom are glimmers of light at the end of the tunnel. They create a more relaxed cultural environment for Afrikaans-speakers. But the possibility of collectively mobilising around a common project seems limited. In this regard, I think one has to look critically at education again, because it builds a bridge between culture and the economy. If we carry on as we have been doing under the current dispensation, there will be no Afrikaans-medium university in ten years' time. Giliomee writes convincingly in this context. Difficult choices will need to be made. It seems sensible to bargain with the government for the survival of at least one Afrikaans-language university. This also offers a common goal that will ensure involvement over a broad ideological and value spectrum. The current rectors will have to decide whether they want an Afrikaans-medium university to survive as a university or as an Afrikaans-language university. These are totally different possibilities. The rectors should not delude themselves, however, that if they choose the former, the latter will follow.

Another result of my fascination with being Afrikaans-speaking is my involvement with Africa as the continent where I live. I have already spoken about this, but currently the involvement manifests to a large extent through the Gorée Institute in Senegal and through the Open Society Initiative for Southern Africa (OSISA). OSISA is primarily active in Zimbabwe, Zambia, Malawi, Angola, Namibia, Botswana, Lesotho, Swaziland and Mozambique. Because

OSISA has to identify projects for funding, it is inevitable that you get caught up in the political, economic and social problems of each country. Angola is on the brink of disintegration; Namibia and Zimbabwe have serious problems of succession; Botswana is peaceful and progressive; Swaziland is peaceful, monarchic and stagnant; Mozambique is recovering; Malawi is struggling to consolidate democratic politics, as is Zambia; and so forth. These insights are gained through the local representatives of OSISA. They all feel, as we do in South Africa, the effects of AIDS slicing through the productive potential of the country like a blade.

One aspect that increasingly fascinates me is the difference in state structures of these countries. Angola is virtually a stateless society. The OSISA contact there is a brave young journalist named Rafael Marques, who was put in solitary confinement for six weeks after writing an article mildly critical of the president. The politics of stateless or virtually stateless societies is much less predictable than that of societies with a functioning state structure. South Africa is far better off in this regard than we realise.

Through my involvement with the Gorée Institute, and through André Zaaiman's intervention, I was invited to visit Jerusalem by a support group for the Israeli Labour Party. It was literally three weeks before the election in which Ehud Barak became prime minister. Meetings were arranged with rightwing Israeli settlers, orthodox Jews, Palestinian intellectuals and Yasser Arafat's party members. The idea was to revive the Oslo Peace Accord if Barak won, and we had to participate to see what the possibilities were for negotiation and mediation between Palestinians and Israelis. They were particularly interested in South Africa's negotiating process and my experience, before this, with the Metropolitan Chamber.

I'd far prefer to have the problems of Africa and South Africa than those of the Middle East, Israel and Palestine. In Jerusalem, my secular scepticism was reinforced when I saw how, within shouting distance of each other, representatives of the greatest monotheistic religions prayed in their respective temples for each other's demise. The hate is almost tangible, and the interaction between Jews and Palestinians at street level in Ramallah, Bethlehem and Jerusalem reminds one of the worst periods of apartheid oppression. Barak deserves every bit of support he can obtain, locally and internationally, to get the Oslo Accord back on track.

So far I have talked mostly about non-income-generating preoccupations. But one has also to earn a living and pay for the groceries. After I left active party politics, I initially started doing political consultancy work and since 1990 I have been a full-time apprentice businessman. The friendship, partnership and wisdom of Jürgen Kögl have been indispensable. He came to see me in early 1990. He was then in his early thirties, a broker, and he wanted us to devise a plan to bring about greater black corporate participation in the country's economy. He believed, correctly, that if this did not happen we would have a difficult time ahead of us. The idea was to bring black politicians and business leaders together to discuss the problem.

We met a few times in the Carlton Hotel: Thabo Mbeki, Oscar Dhlomo, Sam Motsuenyane, Don Mkhwanazi, Mzi Khumalo and others, roughly twenty of us altogether. Eventually it was decided that there was a need for a black investment fund which would buy out medium and smaller productive companies with black majority shareholding, but where white management skills were retained to train the new black management until it could take over and control and manage black companies. There was great enthusiasm for this and Jürgen, Mkhwanazi, Khumalo and I went to all the main financial institutions – Old Mutual, Sanlam, Anglo American, Barlow Rand, and so forth – to discuss the concept. Everywhere the idea was welcomed with great enthusiasm, but nobody grabbed for their cheque books. Eventually, Michael Katz, a tax lawyer, took up the idea and together with Nthato Motlana and Jonty Sandler, and with the help of Sanlam, they took over Metropolitan Life and started the first black empowerment company. This was how New Africa Investments Limited (NAIL) was born. It was precisely the opposite of what we had had in mind. Here there was financing from the major financial institutions for a few black shareholders without any significant transfer of knowledge, while profit remained dependent on the existing white-controlled companies. It had great propaganda value for the furthering of black participation in the corporate life of the South African economy, but I am still not sure how much empowerment it really brought about. There is no doubt that it did make a few people rich very quickly and with very little effort.

After our failed attempt, a few of us decided to scale down the process and privatised. So Khula Investments was established and my consultancy company merged with it. *Khula* is the Zulu word for 'growth'. There were five of us, with equal shareholdings: Mzi Khumalo (later of Johannesburg Consolidated Industries), Max Maisela (now chairman of the Post Office), Khehle Shubane (later co-chairman with me of the task group that arranged the local government elections), Jürgen Kögl and myself. We decided that, in terms of investments, we would focus on the media. This happened partially as a result of my involvement as chairman of the Independent Media Diversity

Trust (IMDT). The aim of this trust was to help so-called community publications and alternative newspapers to survive. But this was not the original intention.

Initially I was asked to participate in a discussion about the establishment of an independent media trust. This was at the home of Pat Retief, then chairman of JCI, which owned the Argus group of newspapers. The idea was that these papers be transferred to the trust to achieve two goals: to make them less vulnerable ideologically as possessions of Anglo American, and to prevent them from being bought out by 'hostile' investors or competitors like Tony O'Reilly or Conrad Black. It was especially feared that the Argus group would become the target of a future ANC government. Nothing came of this initial discussion, however, except that Doug Band and Michael Spicer, both from Anglo American, were approached by a group of editors and journalists of the so-called alternative press who asked for financial assistance. Band and Spicer then approached me and said they wanted to establish an independent trust, which would basically be a funding mechanism for community papers and magazines. With promises of regular financial contributions from the large media companies I was approached to be chairman. The great media groups each gave a few hundred thousand rand and then were no longer interested.

From its inception, the IMDT has been faced with difficulties. Under the old dispensation considerable foreign funding was available for so-called alternative papers at a community or national level. Many of these had been active in their opposition to apartheid, for example *New Nation, Vrye Weekblad* and *Die Suid-Afrikaan*. During that period I was very involved with the latter two, which both did outstanding work. Max du Preez was especially courageous in his exposure of corruption and abuse under the former regime.

With the new order, funding dried up. It was felt that there were more urgent issues than newspapers in trouble, so the money vanished. The simple, hard truth of the matter was that unless a newspaper was financially self-sufficient, it could only be kept alive through massive foreign funding. This was how *Vrye Weekblad, Die Suid-Afrikaan, New Nation* and others vanished from the scene. After a while I resigned from the IMDT and got involved full-time with Khula.

My experiences with the IMDT made me aware of investment opportunities in the press, and so Khula, with more courage than good sense, and even less money, decided to go after the Argus group and its papers. Terry Moolman of Caxton/CTP heard of us and suggested that we pursue the Argus group together. Moolman's group had a hundred times more money than we did, so Khula decided to join forces with Caxton/CTP. I was totally unaware of the bad blood between Anglo and Moolman, who were then in court over mutual trade restrictions, and started negotiating, in good faith, with Julian Ogilvie Thompson, chief executive of the Anglo group, about the acquisition of the Argus group. My naïveté knew no bounds. Moolman and I were convinced that our Afrikaans label would be too difficult for the top guys of Anglo to digest. I even discussed the transaction with Harry Oppenheimer over lunch at the Ritz Hotel in Paris, blissfully unaware that negotiations between Anglo and Tony O'Reilly's Independent group to purchase the Argus group had already reached an advanced stage. Oppenheimer was too much of a gentleman to tell me I was wasting my time.

After Khula's failed attempt to take over the Argus group with Caxton/CTP, Moolman suggested that we should jointly tender for the contract to print telephone directories. In the past this tender usually went to Perskor and/or Nasionale Pers. Perhaps, under the new order, there was now a chance for another company.

Through constant hard work, Moolman and Noël Coburn built Caxton/CTP up from scratch to become a company which by the mid-1990s was capitalised at more than R3 billion. They also owned the latest, most modern printing press in South Africa. We believed that, if we approached the matter strategically, we could win the tender to print telephone directories. The tender was worth several million rands annually. Khula decided to join forces with the Women's Development Bank and then to tender jointly with Caxton/CTP for the telephone directories. We formed a new company, CTP Directories, in which Caxton/CTP had a sixty per cent share, and the Women's Bank and Khula twenty per cent each. The Women's Bank concentrates on the economic emancipation of women, specifically rural black women, with the help of micro-loans for small businesses. We persuaded Caxton/CTP that, as part of our tender and partnership, it should train black women to work the printing presses. Our tender was successful, and after three years the Women's Bank walked away with quite a few million rand, as did Khula.

Moolman was so pleased with Khula's contribution to the telephone directory tender that he lent us money to buy shares in Adcorp Holdings, a 'soft' financial services company, which focuses on personnel recruitment for the private sector and the state, commercial research and industrial advertising. Moolman also invested in it and the investments were very successful.

The business world is not for softies and one has to be wide awake to avoid being outfoxed. One thing I have learnt through experience is that those who speak so glibly about 'fat cats' and merciless businessmen are usually people who have never tried to make money as entrepreneurs. It is extremely hard work with full-time, inherent risks. Both companies of which I am chairman consist of smaller companies started from scratch by small-scale entrepreneurs who risked a great deal and worked hard to be successful.

There is, for example, a middle-aged nursing sister who resigned from her post as matron of a hospital and single-handedly, without capital and with a mortgage on her house, started a venture to place nurses part time on a contract basis at private hospitals. Today, she and her company place three thousand nurses per month and the business is still growing. Two young graduates started an initiative, without money or infrastructure, but with plenty of debt, to provide the private sector with temporary staff. After twenty-five years this initiative has grown into one of the largest recruitment companies in South Africa. One journalist started his own community newspaper in the platteland and grew it into a successful business, which was eventually bought by Caxton/CTP for a hefty amount. These people know hardship and hard work; they have received nothing free. And they have provided work for thousands of others. I am convinced that if South Africa's economy survives, it will be because a favourable climate was created for smaller and medium-sized enterprises like these to thrive. This is where genuine job creation happens, not so much through the state or giant conglomerates.

This is the here and now. I am, in accordance with all objective measures, a failed academic, a failed politician, an apprentice businessman and an exceptionally privileged human being. My children have work, are happy and love me. Jane from Swaziland is my companion, my wife, my partner and my comfort. My brain still functions and I can entertain myself full time with my own thoughts. So far I am not yet so bored that I no longer care, and I know that, as has happened in my life up to now, something new will come along to surprise me once again. This is probably true of most people, in any country. I don't know. All I do know is that in this country and on this continent I still have so much to discover and experience that I do not feel like walking away to start all over again somewhere else.